Praise for *The Angel by My Side*

"The partnership between Mike and Dakota was astonishing, humbling, beyond description—and absolutely true. This remarkable story about a man and a dog has volumes to teach us about healing, devotion, and the mysterious and numinous bond of one soul to another. Must-reading for anyone who has ever loved—or been loved—by a dog. For skeptics of the human-animal bond, this book will make you a convert!"

— **Susan Chernak McElroy,** author of *Animals as Teachers and Healers*

▨   ▨   ▨

*"**The Angel by My Side** magnificently showcases how, over the millennia, we've come to find our relationship with pets inextricably woven into not just our health and happiness, but our very survival. Nobody who reads this book will ever look at their own pets the same way again—they're not pets, they're life-support systems cleverly disguised as four-legged family members! Do your pet and yourself a favor: Buy this book, and when you're done reading it, keep it in the medicine cabinet for the next time you need salve for your soul."*

— **Marty Becker, D.V.M.,** veterinary contributor for
Good Morning America, chief veterinary correspondent for Amazon.com, and author of *The Healing Power of Pets*

▨   ▨   ▨

"Get yourself a comfortable chair and a box of tissues, and curl up with this book. As you read this remarkable story, you will come to believe in the human-animal bond, if you didn't already."

— **Sophie Engelhard Craighead,** Chairperson of the Board, Delta Society

The ANGEL
by My Side

Mike Lingenfelter

Hay House Titles of Related Interest

■　　　■　　　■

All of the above are available at your local bookstore, or may be ordered by visiting:
Hay House USA: **www.hayhouse.com**
Hay House Australia: **www.hayhouse.com.au**
Hay House UK: **www.hayhouse.co.uk**
Hay House South Africa: **orders@psdprom.co.za**

The ANGEL
by My Side

The True Story of a Dog Who Saved a Man . . .
and a Man Who Saved a Dog

Mike Lingenfelter
and David Frei

HAY HOUSE, INC.
Carlsbad, California
London • Sydney • Johannesburg
Vancouver • Hong Kong

Published and distributed in the United States by: Hay House, Inc., P.O. Box 5100, Carlsbad, CA 92018-5100 • *Phone:* (760) 431-7695 or (800) 654-5126 • *Fax:* (760) 431-6948 or (800) 650-5115 • www.hayhouse.com • **Published and distributed in Australia by:** Hay House Australia Ltd., 18/36 Ralph St., Alexandria NSW 2015 • *Phone:* 612-9669-4299 • *Fax:* 612-9669-4144 • www.hayhouse.com.au • **Published and distributed in the United Kingdom by:** Hay House UK, Ltd. • Unit 202, Canalot Studios • 222 Kensal Rd., London W10 5BN • *Phone:* 44-20-8962-1230 • *Fax:* 44-20-8962-1239 • www.hayhouse.co.uk • **Published and distributed in the Republic of South Africa by:** Hay House SA (Pty), Ltd., P.O. Box 990, Witkoppen 2068 • *Phone/Fax:* 2711-7012233 • orders@psdprom.co.za • **Distributed in Canada by:** Raincoast • 9050 Shaughnessy St., Vancouver, B.C. V6P 6E5 • *Phone:* (604) 323-7100 • *Fax:* (604) 323-2600

Editorial supervision: Jill Kramer   *Design:* Jenny Richards
Interior photos: Courtesy of Mike Lingenfelter, except where noted

Library of Congress Cataloging-in-Publication Data

Lingenfelter, Michael
  The angel by my side : the true story of a dog who saved a man . . . and a man who saved a dog / Michael Lingenfelter and David Frei.
      p. cm.
  ISBN 1-40190-021-6 (hardcover) • ISBN 1-4019-0058-5 (tradepaper)
  1.   Golden retriever—Texas—Anecdotes. 2.   Service dogs—Texas—Anecdotes.
  3. Lingenfelter, Michael
  4. Human-animal relationships—Texas—Anecdotes. I. Frei, David. II. Title.
      SF429.G63 L55 2002
  636.762'7'09764—dc21

                          2002005926

                  ISBN 1-4019-0058-5

          06 05 04 03   7 6 5 4
              1st printing, September 2002
              4th printing, September 2003

I dedicate this book to my wife, Nancy, for her unending support during my recovery and the writing of this book; and to my children, for their unquestioning belief in Dakota and his power to heal me.

— M.L.

■　　■　　■　　■　　■

This is for my late father, Jerry Frei, who continues to be, as he always was, my spiritual counselor and inspiration.

— D.F.

CONTENTS

PREFACE

"What lies behind us and what lies before us are
tiny matters compared to what lies within us."

— Ralph Waldo Emerson

I am truly blessed to have known Dakota and to watch him live. I saw him work his magic, and he worked it on me.

For more than 30 years, I've had a wonderful life in the world of dogs. My own dogs have enjoyed competitive success and have worked in animal-assisted therapy; and, since 1990, I have personally had the honor of being the television co-host for the Westminster Kennel Club Dog Show on the USA Network.

But nothing I have ever experienced in the world of dogs has impacted my life like the story of Dakota and Mike. It may or may not change *your* life, but I hope that it touches you and shows you just how great our lives can be when we share them in a meaningful way with our wonderful dogs.

I first met Mike and Dakota in 1999, when I was hired as a public relations consultant for Delta Society to produce a video and handle the publicity for their annual awards show for Therapy Animals and

Service Dogs of the Year. Mike and Dakota were one of the winning service-dog teams, so I flew to Dallas to shoot and produce the story. At the time, the story had just begun—Dakota was saving Mike's life, virtually every day—and it was a beautiful story to tell.

Little did I know that I was going to be a part of a very special journey myself. And every step of the way, I continued to see this lesson: It's not what you *teach* your dog, it's what you *learn from* your dog. Dakota was a great teacher and continues to be an inspiration. I'm so lucky to have been touched by him.

— **David Frei,** September 2002

ACKNOWLEDGMENTS

I have no formal training in writing and have never written a book before. My training is in the technical and business world. But in my heart, I know that I was charged by powers far beyond me to write the history of Dakota's work here on Earth. It's my hope that David and I have captured the power and meaning of Dakota's presence, and that readers of this book will understand that he was an angel sent by God to be by my side, and that my life truly was in his "hands." He didn't just help *me,* though—I know many people who met Dakota and were blessed by him and had their lives changed forever. Dakota has presented to the world the power of the human-animal bond and the lesson that God's four-legged creatures have special powers—if we'd just take the time to listen and try to understand them.

Yes, Dakota was with me, in both my heart and my head, during the writing of his book—for there's no way that David or I could have written this book alone.

I must thank Karen Costello and the Greater Houston Golden Retriever Club (GHGRC) for rescuing Dakota. Thanks to Dr. Harold Krug and his staff, and to Dr. Gregory Ogilvie and the countless staff members at Colorado State University for their help in treating

Dakota's cancer. Thanks to Patty Neger at ABC's *Good Morning America*, and to Dr. Marty Becker for arranging for Dakota to go to CSU. Special thanks to all of the people around the world who prayed for Dakota's recovery and sent us e-mails and cards. And thanks to Dick Tansill, Senior Vice President at Parsons Transportation Group, for allowing me (and Dakota) to return to work.

Thank you to Hay House for printing Dakota's story, but most of all, to my editors, Jill Kramer and Shannon Littrell, for being my guides through this mission in my life.

— **Mike Lingenfelter**

▪   ▪   ▪

First and foremost, I thank Mike for sharing Dakota with me and inviting me to help tell their story.

I have a lot of people to thank as well, but I want to start by thanking my own dogs, Teigh and Belle, who teach me about the human-animal bond and unconditional love every day. My life is better because I share it with them.

I'd like to thank all those dog owners who inspired me, who make a difference in people's lives by volunteering with their animals in health-care facilities and at the site of tragedies such as the World Trade Center and Columbine High School. Susan Stone, Karen Lefrak, Cindy Ehlers, Teoti Anderson, Megan Wolf, Buddy Hayes, Maureen Fredericksen, and all of the rest of you out there—you make me want to do more. I hope that this story about Dakota further energizes you and shows people the wonderful things that you do with your animals and with your hearts.

I'd like to thank David Vigliano and Michael Harriott at Vigliano Associates for believing in us, and all the people at Hay House for helping make this book a reality.

Thanks, too, to Ranny Green and Bob Clampett, for their creative input and editing skills.

Thank you to my wife, Cherilyn, whose love for me and dedication to animal-assisted therapy has given me a new understanding of my own humanity and my own spirituality.

And most of all, thanks to God for letting me live this life. As scripture tells us in Job 12:7, "But ask the animals, and they will teach you . . ."

— David Frei

CHAPTER ONE

Mad at the World

"**N**o way. I already have a dog." My psychiatrist, Dr. Attar, was accustomed to hearing me protest anything and everything that she suggested. This was no different. I didn't need a dog—I knew the end was coming for me, and I *wanted* it to. I'd had enough of life like this, and my angry, macho attitude helped me deal with the inevitable.

I had to face it: I was helpless, at the mercy of my weakened heart. I couldn't do anything without medication or doctors' approvals. I couldn't lift anything heavy; I couldn't drive alone. And the doctors had told me that I wasn't going to get better—I was only going to get worse.

And now they wanted me to get a dog? Great.

■   ■   ■

What happened to me? It was only two years ago that I had the world by the tail. I had a wonderful marriage and a beautiful, loving family. I was living the good life in picturesque, sunny Southern California. I had every engineer's dream job, which was challenging and rewarding *and* made me all the money I could ever need.

My specialty was designing and managing construction of communications and control systems for airports and public transportation. I'd been working on the Los Angeles Metro Rail Red Line, a state-of-the-art mass transit project. It was a pressure-packed project (as most of them were), with demanding deadlines and billion-dollar budgets. I was good at my job, but I was also very driven and intense—a true type-A personality thriving under the demands of my profession.

I couldn't work hard enough. I put in long days on location, and spent countless hours working at home on evenings and weekends. Occasionally I could make myself step away from it, but most of the time my job was my life. So it wasn't a shock when I had a major heart attack; the surprising part was that it didn't happen while I was working—I was out bicycling on one of those spectacular California days instead.

I was lucky to survive. And I was even more fortunate to make it through a second heart attack, which happened less than a week later while I was still in the hospital recovering from the first one. I had emergency open-heart surgery, but unfortunately, I was left with exten-sive damage to my heart and unstable angina.

According to the U.S. Department of Health and Human Services, angina is "recurring pain or discomfort in the chest that happens when some part of the heart does not receive enough blood." In other words, when the flow of blood to any part of the heart is temporarily inter-rupted (usually when an artery is blocked), an angina attack or episode results. By comparison, in a heart attack, the blood flow to the heart is suddenly and permanently cut off, which causes permanent damage to the heart muscle. Usually, the chest pain is worse and lasts longer, but this isn't always the case.

For some people, angina might occur in a predictable pattern, which allows them to regulate their activities and be prepared to deal with the attacks. For those reasons, this is known as "stable angina." What I had, however, was "unstable angina," which is highly unpre-dictable. There's no warning—unstable angina attacks don't need stress or physical exertion to set them off, and there's no pattern to their frequency and severity. In either case, angina attacks can gradually get worse and eventually lead to a heart attack.

Angina doesn't necessarily guarantee a heart attack, but it does imply issues of heart disease and an increased risk of heart attack. Nitroglycerin is the most commonly prescribed drug for angina, as it widens the blood vessels and allows for greater blood flow to the heart. Another option for some is surgery, such as coronary bypass or balloon angioplasty, either of which would hopefully improve the blood flow to the heart. In bypass surgery, a blood vessel is grafted on to the blocked artery to create a "bypass" for the blood flow. In angioplasty, a catheter with a tiny balloon at the end is inserted into the artery and inflated briefly to widen any narrowed passageways.

My heart was too weak to go through another surgery, so I had to learn to live with the pain as my unstable angina attacks continued mercilessly. It may have been different in other people, but to me, an angina attack felt as if my chest was being squeezed in a vise. The pain varied, but it often radiated from my chest up into my shoulders, arms, and neck. Actually, it hurt so bad that I couldn't always tell exactly where the worst part of it was coming from.

I had to leave my job and stay at home to rehabilitate—I began my program two months after the surgery. I was a mess when rehab began: I had to relearn my grandchildren's names, and I even had to relearn how to write. Some of this was a result of the heart attacks, and some of it came about from being on life support during open-heart surgery. I thought that I could strengthen my heart through exercise, and I was sure that the harder I pushed myself, the faster I would recover and be able to get back to work. I knew that I could heal myself, and that occasional pain meant I was making progress, so I went about my rehab with the same intensity that I'd had put in to my job. But when the angina laid me flat a few times, my cardiologist made me stop all rehabilitation activities altogether.

I went to see my doctor and demanded to know why he couldn't fix things. After all, I needed to get back to work. But I found out that this was no longer the primary concern—now the question was how long I might stay alive. My cardiologist told me that I wasn't going to get better and that my best option was to continue with a drug regimen that would help relieve the angina. Surgery still wasn't a choice for me, as my heart wasn't strong enough to allow me to survive. I sought out other medical opinions and got the same gloomy prognosis.

The reality hit me hard: I wasn't going to be going back to work, I wasn't going to get better, I was no longer the breadwinner, and I wasn't much of a husband or father either. I felt woefully inadequate and responsible for all of my family's problems. I was miserable, and I was making sure that everyone around me was, too, including the person I loved the most—my wife, Nancy. I was always looking to start some kind of an argument with her, making sure that she didn't enjoy herself. After all, why should she be happy if I wasn't?

It was August of 1992. I was 54 years old, and I felt like my life was over. I was sitting around waiting to die, and I spent the next few months simply vegetating. Those were long days. I took pills to get up, pills to stay up, and pills to go to bed. I had no hope and no life. Every day I drove Nancy the few blocks to her office, and picked her up at lunch and at the end of the workday. Even though I shouldn't have been driving, I wanted to share my desolation with her.

After a year of this routine—and why she put up with it for that long, I'll never know—we decided to make a change. Nancy retired from her job; and we moved to Katy, Texas, in April of 1993. This was ostensibly to be closer to our children and grandchildren, but deep down inside, I thought that Nancy wanted to have some occasional relief from dealing with my gloomy attitude. One bonus was that being in a Houston suburb put us conveniently near the country's best medical care. After our move, when I wasn't sitting home being impossible to live with, I was spending a lot of time at Houston's Methodist

Hospital. And as if my heart trouble wasn't enough, pulmonary disease and stress-related anxiety were complicating things further—together, all of this was pushing me to thoughts of suicide. This was why I'd been seeing a psychiatrist.

■   ■   ■

When I told Dr. Attar that I didn't want another dog, she ignored me, as she usually did. She always made me so mad. Some of that anger came from the medication I was taking, but most of it just stemmed from being a raging, frustrated, type-A, macho fool. Since being angry was my only defense, I used it quite often with her. I knew that I was going to die—Dr. Attar couldn't do anything about that, and neither could I. And I didn't care. In fact, I was planning to help the process along. If I could have been sure that my death would have left Nancy with enough money to take care of herself or wouldn't have made the insurance companies ask any questions, I would have ended it in a minute and freed her from her burdens.

Dr. Attar knew this. She'd been treating me for depression and anxiety ever since my arrival in Houston, and she heard my anger, threats, depression, and lies every week without fail. During this session, I started to get out of my chair, but she stopped me cold.

"You just sit right there and listen to me," Dr. Attar said. "Dr. Young and I agree on this: You're not making any progress. You're mad at the world, and you're taking it out on everyone around you, especially Nancy," she scolded. "You need to do something that gets you out of the house, something to get you exercising."

I thought my psychiatrist was supposed to make me feel good, not agitate me.

In one of my first visits to see Dr. Young, my cardiologist, I had a severe angina attack in his office. He admitted me to the hospital right away, and afterward, I told him that I wished he would have just let me die. I couldn't understand why he wasted his time with me when he could have been saving someone who deserved his time and effort.

Dr. Attar seemed to know that this is how I really felt, in spite of all my best attempts to mislead her into believing that I was okay. "Mike, we need something to work on your mental healing, too. Dr. Young and I think that a therapy dog just might be the answer."

"Why can't I just use Abbey?" I asked, referring to our golden retriever.

"Nancy thinks that Abbey is too hyper for you. You need a quieter dog," she said.

"I don't need *any* dog," I argued. "I certainly don't need a therapy dog, whatever that is."

Dr. Attar persisted. "You need a diversion. You've got too much time on your hands, and I don't like that. I don't want you quitting on me."

"Yeah, right." I'd already quit, and Dr. Attar knew it. She knew that each week could be her last shot at me.

I had enough energy to give her a sarcastic response: "Sure, I have a lot to live for, don't I? I never get out of bed, and I'm living on pills 24 hours a day."

I'd been spending a lot of time trying to figure out how to end it all peacefully. I had my pilot's license, and I thought about just renting a plane and flying off into the sunset. I had also purchased a gun. And I had all kinds of pills lying around. I knew that I could take a bunch of my antidepressants, or I could just stop taking the heart pills that were keeping me alive—I'd get the desired result either way. What did I have left to live for? I wasn't healthy, my medications weren't doing any good, I couldn't work, I was a burden to my family, my life savings were going down the drain, my marriage was falling apart from the pressure, and I was helpless to do anything about any of it.

"I don't want any more therapy, either from you or some dog. Why don't you all just leave me alone?!" I spat. The truth was, I thought a dog would just get in the way of my plans to end it all.

Dr. Attar read my mind. "Here's your choice: You either go along with this and give it a try, or I'll put you in the hospital right now, where you can be protected from yourself. It's your call."

Well, I may not have been thrilled about how my life was going "on the outside," but I knew that I didn't want to be in any hospital. All the time I had to spend in the doctors' offices was bad enough. I decided that I'd just have to play this game for a while.

"Okay, I'll talk it over with Nancy and we'll figure out how to do this," I told Dr. Attar. But I was really thinking that another dog could just play with Abbey and stay out of my hair.

As I left Dr. Attar's office, I was proud of myself for finally outsmarting her. I admitted to being a lot of things then—bitter, fatalistic, and obstinate all easily came to mind—but I've never been stupid. I'd always had my doctors fully inform me as to what exactly what was going on with my body. I was smart enough to understand what the doctors were telling me, and that's probably *why* I was so mule-headed about my life. So anyway, I wanted to know what this therapy-dog stuff was all about—why were Dr. Attar and Dr. Young suddenly insistent about my getting a dog? Of all people, they should have known that I had my hands full just taking care of myself.

That night, Nancy and I turned to the Internet for some answers to all of the questions we had, such as: What is a therapy dog, what does a therapy dog do, and where do you find one? We found several references to "animal-assisted therapy" and "the human-animal bond," and stories about people visiting nursing homes and schools with their dogs, making senior citizens happy and entertaining kids. There was a continuing theme about the role of animals in improving human health and enhancing the quality of life. Delta Society had a tag line of "Animals helping people, people helping animals." The primary objective of Therapy Dogs International was " . . . to provide comfort and companionship by sharing the dog with the patients in hospitals, nursing homes, and other institutions . . ."

The mission of another therapy-dog organization, The Good Dog Foundation, was to use " . . . professionally trained and supervised adult and animal teams . . . to aid the healing process in humans and enhance their quality of life." Their tag line was, "Because good dogs are good medicine." But the line that really got my attention was on the Delta Website: "Individuals who have mental illness or low self-esteem focus on themselves; animals can help them focus on their environment. Rather than thinking and talking about themselves and their problems, they watch and talk to and about the animals."

"That pretty much says it all right there, doesn't it?" I asked Nancy. "Maybe these doctors aren't so stupid after all." But just because I found out what they were trying to do for me, that didn't mean I had to like it. Being resentful and stubborn, trying to make Nancy suffer, and contemplating suicide all required my full attention. A dog would only complicate things.

But Nancy was already making a plan. After all, like most little-boy-and-their-dog stories, she knew that she'd probably be the one stuck with most of the chores, such as feeding, bathing, and letting the dog out. "I think we should get another golden retriever," she said, "so Abbey can play with it, too."

"This isn't a done deal here," I replied. "I'm still not sure I want another dog. I'm just trying to find out what the doctors are thinking."

Just like Dr. Attar, Nancy ignored me. "And I think that we should look into finding a rescue dog," she said.

A rescue dog? I remember thinking. *Who's going to rescue me?*

We'd been members of the Greater Houston Golden Retriever Club (GHGRC) for the past year or so. We joined when we first came to town, thinking we might find people who shared our interest in that breed, or that we could find "friends" for Abbey. But we found that the club was oriented around dog shows and field trials, and the members really didn't seem to have much interest in us or our dog. But the club's active rescue function got our attention. There are a lot of golden retrievers in this world, and they often end up in shelters for any number of reasons: People move or get a divorce, their lifestyle changes and they no longer have enough time to spend with the dog, there are behavior issues with the dog, the dog gets caught in an abusive situation, or they just aren't working out in their current homes.

In our disposable society, sorry to say, people often just dump the dog in the local shelter to get off the hook. In most shelters, of course, chances are that a dog will end up being euthanized. There just aren't enough homes out there. A lot of purebred dog organizations have taken the initiative to take responsibility for their breeds, and whenever one shows up at the local shelters, or they're abandoned or being mistreated, the dogs are "rescued" by the group, which then tries to find new homes for the animals. Since there are so many golden retrievers, this was a pretty busy activity for the GHGRC. Since we weren't into showing or field trials, Nancy and I (mostly Nancy, of course) dabbled in rescue work for the club, and we even served as a foster home for a couple of dogs temporarily until new homes were found for them.

"Let's call Karen Costello," Nancy said. I started to say something, but she was already dialing.

Nancy reached our friend Karen, who was the rescue chair for the GHGRC. I was listening in on the extension, hoping to find out what she might know about therapy dogs. Nancy told Karen that my doctors had suggested that we find a therapy dog, and that we decided it would be nice if we could find a golden retriever in rescue that might work for us.

Karen knew a little about therapy dogs, and filled in a few of the blanks in our knowledge base. She told us that therapy dogs are individually trained by their owners, and that the training process is varied according to the projected use of the dog. Karen was familiar with Delta

Society and suggested that we look further into what they had to offer in the way of advice and documentation. But she also said that she might have a candidate for us right away.

"Let me tell you about this dog named Dakota."

CHAPTER TWO

Just Like Me

How does a dog end up chained to a stake in someone's backyard in the sweltering Texas heat? Did he eat someone's shoe or chew up a feather pillow? Did he have a housebreaking accident on some pricey new carpet? Or did he just become too expensive all of a sudden? What changed him from a happy, loyal, tail-wagging member of the family to an afterthought and a burden?

Personally, I'll never understand it, but that's how Karen Costello found this young golden-red dog one spring day in Houston in 1994. He was skinny and in poor health, and he looked as if he'd been pretty much ignored for some time.

Karen learned about this dog when she received a call from a woman who claimed that the dog wasn't hers, nor did she know to whom it belonged, but she wanted it gone. If Karen didn't come and get it, the caller said, she'd have it put to sleep. This was the classic "rescue story" that Karen and others in her field often heard—people who wouldn't take responsibility for a bad situation suddenly didn't own the dog; in fact, they didn't know who the owner was, but they were just trying to help. Karen had been working in rescue long enough to know that she was often hearing stories that weren't 100-percent factual. She had no way of knowing what was true and what wasn't—but her job was to save the dog, not judge the people.

Rescue didn't automatically mean a happy ending to a sad story. Sometimes dogs can't be rescued, usually for reasons of health or temperament. Karen was concerned that the dog she saw in front of her might be headed toward one of those unhappy endings, and she'd seen enough of those over the years. There were so many dogs out there that could be saved—but she didn't always have the time or the energy, and the club didn't always have the funds to fix everything.

But as Karen approached this dog, she saw something in his personality and in his eyes. She said a little prayer to herself: "Please, God, help me make this one end with smiles everywhere." Symbolically, it was important to Karen to give a rescued dog a new name whenever she could, which indicated a fresh start. She had one ready for this youngster.

"C'mon, Dakota, let's get out of here," she said softly, as she unfastened the chain and gathered him up. *Dakota* was a Native American word for "friend," and the dog now named as such was wagging his tail for her. Karen smiled—for her, rescue was often about small victories.

Karen placed Dakota in a dog crate in the back of her car and headed off to see her veterinarian. As it turned out, Dakota had heartworm disease, which is spread by mosquitoes. Mosquitoes carry a parasite called *dirofilaria immitis* that lives in the arteries and the heart chambers of dogs. As these parasites multiply, they can create life-threatening blockages in the dog's arteries and heart. Being chained up in a backyard where mosquitoes were abundant—as Dakota had been—would expose a dog to greater risk of becoming infected. Infected dogs can be treated, but the treatment is delicate and can also create fatal blockages, as these worms are killed and carried out of the heart a few at a time.

Karen's veterinarian started the treatment for Dakota right away. Early in the process, however, his heart stopped, probably from a blockage. After some anxious moments, Dakota survived, and the heartworm was eventually eradicated. He was seemingly on the road back to good health and that happy ending Karen had hoped for.

Because of his personality, the rescue people decided that Dakota would make a good service-dog candidate, so they donated him to the Texas Service and Hearing Dogs organization. Dakota passed all of the required temperament tests and began the program. But after a couple of months of training, a routine hip x-ray revealed an old injury, which apparently went untreated at the time it occurred. It was impossible to know exactly how it may have happened, but the ball of his femur had been driven through his hipbone. Maybe Dakota had been hit by a car or suffered some other trauma during his puppyhood. The cause didn't really matter, but Dakota ended up failing his physical exam. It was amazing that he almost made it through the entire training program before his broken hip was noticed.

The school sent him back to Karen, and she placed him in a foster home with a club member while the GHGRC decided what to do next. Dakota didn't seem to be in any pain, but he still needed to have hip surgery to prevent future suffering and arthritis. It would be an expensive procedure, and the club wasn't able to pay for it.

When Karen spoke to Nancy and me about this dog, she said, "This guy was an x-ray away from being a service dog. Why don't you go visit Dakota at his foster home, and if you think you'd like to get to know him a little better, take him home for the weekend. He's probably very well prepared to be a therapy dog for you—but he does come with a pretty extensive medical file."

That made me smile. "Well, so do I," I told her. "And my heart stopped, too, just like his did." I was surprising myself. It almost sounded as if I was looking for reasons for this to happen.

"I can't make any promises," Karen said. "But if it does work out between you, then you'll need to get him that hip surgery."

That night, Nancy and I drove down to southwest Houston to see Dakota. We took Abbey with us—after all, she was a part of this, too.

Foster homes for rescue dogs can be hard to find, and you never know when someone with their heart in the right place was trying to do more than they really could, either physically or mentally. We were trying not to be judgmental, but we were a little put off by the fact that Dakota was living in a crate in this person's kitchen.

Nancy didn't like that at all, for it seemed as if Dakota was being held, not "homed," as rescue people like to say. "I guess it's better than being at the shelter," she said to me quietly.

Dakota's foster "parent" opened the door of the crate to let him out. At first, he seemed a little subdued and wary of us. This struck us as a bit unusual, since most golden retrievers act like your best friend as soon as they see you.

Dakota glanced around the room and then went directly to Abbey and gave her a little growl. Then he moved to Nancy, and his tail started wagging slowly. He looked at me for about two seconds—he was smart enough to know which of us he had to win over, so he went back to the girls.

He didn't make much of a first impression on me. I didn't particularly like him, and there was just something about him that bugged me. He growled again softly at Abbey, but she kept after him, and soon they were tolerating one another in sort of a kid-like, "This-is-my-toy-and-you-can't-have-it" standoff.

I don't think Nancy was overly nuts about him, but she *did* like him. And it was readily evident that Abbey wasn't going to be an issue. Dakota eventually spent some time working on me, bringing me this green rubber frog he had over and over again. Now that I'd seen him in action, I could understand why he was kept in that crate. I wasn't convinced just yet that Dakota was *the* dog, this therapy dog of destiny that Dr. Attar had in mind for me.

"Let's bring him home," she said. "Let's get him out of here—we could at least give him a break for a couple of nights, anyway."

"That really isn't what we're doing here," I said. "We're not here to save him; we're here to see if he's the right dog for us." I didn't receive an answer to my protest, so I reluctantly consented and led him to the car.

The drive home was an adventure. Dakota was totally obnoxious—he spent the trip vying with Abbey for our attention and protecting his green frog from everyone.

"There's no way we're keeping this dog," I told Nancy. "In fact, let's just turn around and take him back right now."

"We'll talk about it in the morning," she said, in the tone that I had come to recognize as meaning that the discussion was over. I think she was feeling sorry for the dog. I was feeling sorry for myself . . . as usual. All of that notwithstanding, one thing was obvious in the confined space of the car—Dakota desperately needed a bath before he could come into our house. So when we got home, even though it was dark out, we gave him a bath in the driveway—just what I wanted to do at 10 o'clock at night. That earned Dakota another mark in my "bad dog" column.

We finally got him in the house, and I had to admit that he acted happy to be there. His eyes seemed to light up a bit, and he became more personable than he'd been at his foster home. But that green frog was going to be the death of me—whenever he wanted something, he came over and shoved it in my face. And when he saw all of Abbey's toys, it was suddenly Christmas for golden retrievers. Dakota spent the evening bringing those to me and shoving them in my face, too. I was tired, I wanted to go to sleep, and he was making me nuts.

Nancy seemed to be enjoying the entertainment. He wasn't bothering her as much as he was me. It was as if he was targeting me because he knew he'd already won her over.

But I decided that I simply could not deal with this dog. "This is going to be a pretty short trial period," I told Nancy. "This is the most obnoxious animal I've ever been around." I felt that the chemistry between us just wasn't right. "We're taking him back. I know that he's supposed to keep me occupied and moving around, but this is just ridiculous. He's constantly in my face with that stupid frog."

"Just give him some time to get used to you," Nancy told me. "There doesn't need to be a big rush here."

I wasn't buying that. "I can't take it—let's get him out of here. He's going to give me another heart attack."

But Nancy persisted. "This dog has been through a lot, Mike. He's had a bad heart, people have given up on him, and he keeps getting one more chance to survive. Does that sound familiar? He's just like you."

Just like me? Oh, my God. She was right. Dakota *was* just like me—bad heart and all. I looked at him, and I looked at her. "Okay," I said. "I'll give him one more day, but that's it."

■　■　▨　■　▨

CHAPTER THREE

The Green Rubber Frog

The green frog was still on the floor of my living room . . . which meant that his four-legged buddy was around here somewhere, too. When I went to bed the night before, I really didn't want Dakota in my life. But, as I tried to fall asleep, I couldn't shake the last words I'd heard from Nancy: *"He's just like you."*

Maybe that's the reason Dakota looked a little different to me as I wandered into the kitchen for my morning coffee. He was lying in the middle of the family room, with most of Abbey's toys piled up in front of him. When he saw me, he wagged his tail but didn't move. I tried not to look at him so that I could avoid having that green frog shoved in my face.

Nancy set a cup of coffee down in front of me. "I think he's been waiting for you," she said. "He's been watching the hallway all morning, and even now, his eyes haven't left you."

Uh-oh. *Don't look at him, don't look at him, don't look at him . . .* I couldn't help myself. I snuck a peek at him, and he was on me in a split second—how about a little frog with your coffee?

"Good morning, Dakota," I sighed, stroking his ears as he chewed the frog right in my lap.

I'd thought about his heart problems and what he'd been through as I fell asleep the previous night. How about that? Normally I was too busy being angry and feeling sorry for myself to ever think about anyone else's problems. I remembered what Delta Society's Website said: *Animals can help individuals with low self-esteem by placing the focus on the animals rather than themselves.* That's exactly what was happening with Dakota and me—I was thinking about him, not myself.

However, I still wasn't convinced that we could make a connection. In fact, part of the reason that I'd even let the situation get this far is because I wanted to get Dr. Attar off my back, to show her that *no* dog was going to be able to help me. I hated to admit that she might have been right . . . but I wasn't ready to return him to his foster home either.

"How's Abbey dealing with him?" I asked Nancy.

"They already love each other," she said. "She brought him every toy of hers that he didn't already have. I think they're still setting up boundaries, but there won't be any issues with her if he stays."

I tossed the frog across the room, and Dakota brought it right back to me. His tail hadn't stopped wagging all morning. I looked at Nancy. "Did you talk to Karen yet?" I asked.

"No, but we should probably give her a call and let her know how it's going," she said, with sort of a question mark at the end, as if she wanted to hear my take on it.

Dakota set the frog in my lap and then pushed at me with his nose. I tossed it again, and he brought it back. I was sure that there could be no end to this. He looked me right in the eye, and I looked back. Dogs tend to use their eyes to establish dominance, but Dakota's were inviting . . . and I saw something special in them. I wasn't sure what it was, but I wondered if I might see it again. I thought back to that dog crate in the kitchen where we found him. I looked over at the pile that Dakota had made of Abbey's toys, and then I looked at him.

"How about you?" I asked Nancy. "Are you ready to take care of one more of us?"

Nancy had a startled look on her face—and my words had surprised *me* just as much.

"I've got nothing to do with it," she said, her face breaking into a grin. "You know what Dr. Attar said: Dakota's all yours, buddy." Her look told me that she was helping to make this happen . . . and she was loving every minute of it.

That morning, Dakota and I went for our first walk together. As we roamed through the neighborhood, he looked and sniffed at everything, and wagged his tail the entire time. It was pretty quiet out there, and we only went to the end of the block and back. But in that short time, I could easily see that Dakota was very special.

When we got back to the house, I told him, "We're home." Just like that, I had fallen in love with Dakota, and he was here to stay. I called Karen to tell her he was staying, and she told me that she'd absolutely known that the home Dakota needed would be with Nancy and me.

■   ■   ■

It was pretty simple at first. Dakota figured out right away that if he brought the squeaking green frog over and put it in my face, he was assured to get what he wanted. It got to the point that I didn't even have to see the silly thing—I'd just hear it squeak and I'd grab the leash and head for the door, where Dakota was already waiting. He also used the frog to get me to feed him, to let him out in the backyard, and to get me to pull a toy out from under the couch. He could go from obnoxious to loyal and loving at a moment's notice, and return back to obnoxious just as quickly. He had a good thing going, and here I thought *he* was supposed to be working for *me*.

But to be fair, he did take care of me, too. When I wasn't feeling well, he could tell. He'd climb into bed with me and comfort me, lying quietly beside me for hours at a time. I was still having heart issues, (particularly angina attacks), and Dakota would help me work through the pain. He wouldn't let me get upset or angry about anything anymore—he'd come to me, demand my attention, and distract me from whatever was bothering me. This was a great blessing for Nancy, who was the usual target of my anger.

I was seeing the basic concepts of animal-assisted therapy that we'd read about on the Internet. I understood how having Dakota around was helping me relax and take my mind off whatever the moment might have been bringing me, whether it was pain, stress, or depression. I was too busy tending to Dakota to spend any time feeling sorry for myself or thinking about suicide. And much of this therapy consisted of physical activity—throwing the ball or tossing the frog to him, petting him, roughhousing with him, bathing him, or brushing him. All of this was good activity for me.

Even though I had my own four-legged physical therapist (and psychotherapist) at home, I continued to visit Dr. Attar. Yet these sessions were much different than they'd been previously. Instead of focusing on my anger and hopelessness, I talked to her about Dakota and me, how we were getting along, and the things we did together. I found myself looking forward to my visits with Dr. Attar, and I was having fun sharing Dakota with her and everyone else. Dakota was bringing me out of my shell and returning me back to my real self.

Our short walks to the end of the block got longer—pretty soon we were covering the entire neighborhood. People started to look for us. If we missed seeing someone one day, the next day they were waiting for us, wanting to know what had happened. Nancy and I took care of Dakota's hip surgery in August, and he and I consequently had to miss several days of our neighborhood walk. Well, we must have told and retold what had happened to him a thousand times. And somehow, his rehabilitation became my physical and mental therapy. We continued to meet people, talking to them about Dakota and his role in my life. It was no surprise that I began to talk more about

Dakota and less about myself.

My life had definitely changed. Within six months, Dr. Attar took me off of my anxiety medications, and I was fully functional and enjoying my newfound life with "Cody," as I nicknamed him. We were living a life lesson here: When you share your joy, it multiplies; when you share your pain, you cut it in half. As I look back on it now, I was just beginning to realize who had really rescued whom.

A lot of the fun of being with Cody was just watching him be a dog, enjoying how he lived in the here-and-now without fretting over the past or worrying about the future. He was *living* life moment-by-moment, and he was thankful for every second of it. I loved that about him, and I hoped that I could learn how to be that way, too.

■   ■   ■

It was spring of 1995, more than three years since my first heart attack. Before Dakota, I thought that my next venture out into the world would be for my own funeral. But now, he was getting me out every day, and I was really enjoying it. I loved how he brought that personality of his everywhere we went.

Someone once said that if dogs could talk, they'd say, "Me, too, me, too!" That's absolutely the golden retriever's approach to life. It's as if they're constantly saying:

"What are we going to do now?"

"Where are we going today?"

"What's that you're eating?"

"That sunshine feels great!"

"Here, throw this ball."

"Who's here?"

Cody always had that golden-retriever gleam in his soft, dark eyes, as if he was smiling and rather pleased with himself. It was a look that could make anybody grin and forget (at least for a moment) what their problems might be. In fact, I wish that there was some way to keep count of the number of smiles this dog evoked in others.

His luscious reddish-gold hair was beautiful . . . whether it was on him or on our clothes or furniture. And his tail was always wagging. They say that dogs smile with their tails, and I wouldn't argue with that. Cody had one of those tails that cleared its own path and made you think twice about putting anything breakable or spillable on the coffee table.

His daily belly-flop dives and dog-paddling skills in our backyard pool would have made him the pride of any canine Olympic swim team. Oh, yes, there was always some of that red hair in the pool filter, too. Whenever I cleaned it out, I just reminded myself that Cody was giving me more physical therapy for my heart, and that was good for me.

He only had one green frog, but it seemed like there were a dozen— I was constantly finding "them" in my chair, on the couch, in the hall-way, on our bed, and in the bathroom. And anytime I wasn't stepping on the frog or removing it from the furniture, he was pushing it into my face, wanting to play.

Every day, I was seeing what Dakota could do, not just for me, but for everyone we met on our daily adventures. I was intrigued by the impact he was having and found myself inspired to do more. There real-ly was something to this animal-assisted therapy (AAT). I dove into the topic on the Internet, and made a few phone calls to learn more.

Karen Costello had suggested that I take Dakota through the Canine Good Citizen (CGC) test, which is administered by the American Kennel Club (AKC). This program stresses responsible pet ownership and basic good manners in public for dogs. I was pretty sure that, like a lot of our activities, this was something that people told me was for the dog, but was really for me.

I called the AKC and got the details of the test, and Cody and I practiced every day, both at home and on our walks. It was good thera-py for me, and it helped us build a working relationship. He made everything seem so easy that I was concerned we weren't doing something right. *Isn't this supposed to be tougher?* I wondered.

We decided to take the test at the Houston Kennel Club dog show later that summer. The night before the show, I couldn't sleep. I was very nervous—it was virtually my first venture out of the house in almost four years, other than to doctors' offices or on our neighborhood walks.

It was probably good for us that we were supposed to be tested at 9 A.M. I hadn't even thought that there would be spectators there, but they were lined up around the ring when we got there. Dakota took it all in stride. He was the first in the ring and went through it like he'd been doing this all of his life. He breezed through all of the obstacles: Greeting strangers? He's never met a stranger and probably never will. Strange noises? He never moved a muscle. Unfamiliar dogs? He never missed a beat. He could have been the poster dog for the CGC program. He got a perfect score, something that the CGC testers had never seen before.

As I was gathering up our paperwork, a lady came up to me and said, "Hi, I'm Jan Hassler, and I'm the director for Paws for Caring. We have a booth right over there. Would you please come and see us before you leave?"

"Sure," I said. "What's 'Paws for Caring'?"

"We work with animal-assisted therapy."

"We'll be right there."

Jan had watched Dakota in the ring, and she told me that his temperament was perfect for AAT work and she would like to help get us involved. I told her that I'd been gleaning information about AAT wherever I could, and we had our own little AAT operation going in my neighborhood, but it was really time for me to talk to a live person about it.

She smiled knowingly. "Well, you've seen just a tiny little bit of what you can accomplish. I think you can touch a lot of people in a meaningful way if you come along with us," she said.

It was absolutely perfect timing for us to meet, and we had a great visit. Jan told me about the accomplishments of the people and animals that were part of the organization, and about the places that their members went to each week. I was hooked. Dakota would be a natural, and I was excited to add an activity like this to my life. The next step was to become AAT-certified, which we could do through Paws for Caring, under the guidelines of Delta Society's Pet Partners program.

I had become good friends over the telephone with Susan Duncan at Delta, and she was encouraging Dakota and me every step of the way. It was nice to know that Susan and the people at Delta would be there for us as we began this journey. In addition, Delta's certification process teaches guidelines and standards for bringing animals to health-care facilities and schools, and also provides $1 million in liability insurance.

The test itself was sort of an expanded version of the CGC test, simulating the situations that a volunteer and his animal partner might be exposed to in a health-care facility. For instance, someone came up behind us and dropped a bedpan on the floor. I jumped, but Dakota hardly moved. "Patients" (role-playing volunteers) in wheelchairs and walkers surrounded us, and Cody just sat there, counting new friends. More role players posed as noisy, disoriented adults and rowdy children, getting in our faces and tugging at Dakota. I wanted to pull him away, but he just sat there and took it—more often than not, he even wagged his tail.

Cody kept looking at me, as if to ask, "Are we done yet?" He was solid and dependable, and never wavered. Once again, this test wasn't much of a challenge for him, and I'm sure that I was much more nervous than he was. However, I must not have held him back too much because we passed with flying colors. We were ready to start visiting. But before we went to work, I wanted to know more about animal-assisted therapy. I did a little research and found that it has its roots in the very simple fact that *animals make our lives better.*

Tens of thousands of years ago, wolves began to show up at the campfires of humans, looking for food. This was the beginning of a relationship that has lasted and thrived ever since. Over the years, those wild wolves evolved into domesticated dogs (cats joined the family later), and they were put to work for people—doing everything from serving as security to pulling a sled to ridding farms and homes of rats and pests. Occasionally, animals have even performed extraordinary, heroic acts—such as waking a family in time to save them from a fire, or protecting them from wild animals or criminals.

And along the way, the added bonus of loving companionship has enhanced that human-animal bond. In the simplest terms, it's been a "feel-good relationship": We pet our dog or our cat, or we talk to our bird, or we go horseback riding, and we feel better. For all of these years, seemingly simple acts with our companion animals have made us smile, forget our problems, and feel a little better. That was it in layman's terms, and no one really looked for a deeper explanation.

About 200 years ago, a Quaker group in England used animals to help patients in asylums learn to cope with everyday life. But animal-assisted therapy wasn't really documented until World War II, when hospitals used animals to help members of the armed forces recover from the physical and mental aspects of injuries and trauma. However, there wasn't much scientific basis cited in the work; it was simply observed that animals helped people feel better, whether it was at home or in a health-care facility.

The first service dogs came on the scene about 70 years ago as guide dogs for the blind. Subsequently, service dogs have been trained through the years to become involved in other functions as well, such as seizure alerts, hearing assistance, mobility assistance, and physical support. The role and the benefits of service dogs were self-evident: These animals allowed their people to go back to work and return to a mainstream way of life, which provided the emotional support and dignity that had been absent from the individuals' lives. But service dogs require extensive training, and their use is limited to a specialized function and to people with specific disabilities.

Animal-assisted therapy began to get serious attention some 25 years ago. The progress of recovering patients was often enhanced by interactions with animals, and therapists and health-care workers began to document it. Animals were helping patients recover from strokes or deal with disabilities—range of motion could be regained by petting a cat, throwing a ball to a dog, or taking a step toward an eager animal in order to feed it a treat.

The motivation to interact with an animal was often greater than when one simply responded to a therapist's instructions—this was particularly true with children. The mental and spiritual benefits included verbal interaction, paying attention, improving self-esteem, and relieving anxiety and loneliness. When a pet was involved, patients tended to interact more with others. And animals could provide the learning basis for vocabulary, memory, and concepts such as size and color. Simple grassroots studies showed that having a pet could help lower blood pressure, and that seniors who own dogs make fewer visits to the doctor than those who don't.

The success of animal-assisted therapy is based on the idea that our animals are nonjudgmental and make great listeners, and they offer unconditional, tail-wagging love. In other words, smiles, conversations, and memories evoked by our animals really do provide healing moments.

■　　■　　■　　■　　■

CHAPTER FOUR

We Can Make a Difference

I knew that Dakota and I could make a difference for people in need. My own confidence was slowly returning, and my fears were lessening—I was beginning to feel that I could be useful and independent once again. This was the first task of any magnitude that I'd undertaken since my heart attacks and surgery, and, while Dr. Attar and Nancy were excited for me and supportive, they had to remind me to watch for signs of fatigue and be mindful of my health. I was still battling angina attacks and other health problems, so I had to pace myself in any activities I undertook.

One of the first places Dakota and I visited was the Shriners Hospital for Children, and our time there would come to have the greatest impact on me. The unconditional love of a dog did much to repair the emotional and physical issues of the patients and their families, which had been brought on by radical surgery and life-threatening diseases.

Cody was stronger than I was when it came to dealing with these kids. I found it almost unbearable to think of a child having to face such challenges—nor could I even begin to understand the families' own problems, from trying to battle the pain of the child, to dealing with their own guilt for not being able to do more, to trying to imagine the uncertain future that they all faced. But Cody and I tried to do what we could to help these kids and their families.

Technically, the term for what Dakota and I were doing is "animal-assisted activities and therapy" (Delta Society calls it "AAA/T"). In the "activities" part of the therapy, the animals visit and help cheer up patients and families, while perhaps taking their minds off their troubles. The theory is simple: Petting and interacting with an animal helps ease a person's troubles and lowers their blood pressure, and often hastens their recovery process.

In animal-assisted therapy, the animals and their handlers work under the direction of a physician, nurse, or therapist (physical, speech, occupational, and the like) in a planned program for individual patients, which can be physical, emotional, or spiritual in its nature and goals. The idea may be to get a patient to move a specific body part—for example, using their arm to throw a toy for a dog to retrieve, brush a cat, or even to simply stroke an animal. Or patients might be prompted to take a step or walk over to an animal and give him a treat. Perhaps the animal serves to motivate a person to speak or learn something, such as reading or drawing. And any of these activities may figure in to the patient's emotional and spiritual healing, which is just as important as their physical rehabilitation.

We always encountered a little bit of everything at the Shriners Hospital, and Dakota could handle it all. For instance, little Linda was seven years old and had gone through surgery to remove her cancerous right leg. The nurse on the floor had told me that Linda was in a great deal of pain, and she was confused and emotionally spent.

I took a deep breath as Cody led me into the room. Linda's mother and father were sitting alongside the bed, and they stood to greet us. I saw Linda smile, which was enough for me right there—I was already fighting back the tears.

"Oh, look, Linny—a dog!" said her mother. "Isn't he beautiful?"

Linda nodded.

"Would you like to pet him?" I asked, still trying not to burst into tears.

She nodded again.

I brought him alongside the bed, where she could pet him. "His name is Dakota," I told her.

"Hi, Dakota."

"He loves to visit here," I said. "He loves it when the children smile at him."

Linda's parents were smiling, and Dakota seemed to be, too, as he softly wagged his tail. I could tell that he knew Linda was hurting.

"Do you have a dog at home, Linda?" I asked her.

"No, we have a cat."

"Well, how about if we share Dakota while you're here?"

"Okay," she said, smiling wider.

Dakota stood up on his hind legs, placing his front paws on Linda's bed. I was still new to this and wasn't exactly sure what to do, but I shortened his leash and kept him from getting too close.

Linda's dad took charge. "Look, Linny, he wants to get up there with you," he reassured her.

"He gets into bed with me sometimes when I'm not feeling well," I said, "but my bed is a little bigger than yours. How about if we just put him next to you in a chair?"

"Okay." She was still smiling, and her eyes were getting bigger and brighter. If eyes are indeed the windows to the soul, Linda was showing us that her soul was feeling some much-deserved contentment.

It wasn't a work of art, but I pulled a chair next to the bed and lifted Cody's rear end into it. I put a towel on the bed, and he put his front paws and upper body on it next to Linda. As she petted away, he just lay there quietly.

"We haven't seen her smile like this since she got here," her mother said, her voice choked with emotion.

"And *we* haven't smiled too much either," added her father. "She's on the maximum amount of pain medication that her system can bear, and they won't give her any more. I think that this might just be the next best thing for her."

We didn't talk much after that—we stood there quietly and took in the moment, watching Linda pet Cody until she eventually fell asleep. I gently lifted him off his chair, and we went out in the hall, where I proceeded to hug him. Then I sank my face deep into his soft red fur and wept.

■   ■   ■

Physical therapy can be a long, tedious process, one that's dominated by repetition and pain. It can be difficult to convince the patient to push themselves, to go through all the motions over and over, and have the commitment to persevere.

A lot of health-care professionals will tell you that they find it easier to motivate their patients, especially children, when an animal is present. A physical therapist once told me that having Dakota there almost always made things happen immediately for her patients, instead of taking two or three days to accomplish. A dog like Dakota could liven up the normal routine of the day: When he interacted with patients, his tail would wag, he'd plant big wet kisses on their faces, and smiles and laughter would fill the room. It wasn't work for the patient—it was a happy experience.

For instance, instead of instructing someone to walk, the therapist might say, "Take this cookie over to Dakota." To get them to move their arm, the therapist could say, "Throw this ball for Dakota," and so on.

And the patient's response would turn from, "I don't want to," to "Yes, I can."

I've seen children take their first step in the rehabilitation process because of Cody. I've heard stroke patients say their first full sentence in response to a question about him, after weeks of one-word answers. I've seen kids smile who had nothing to smile about before this dog got there, and believe me, that emotional lift is as important to the healing process as anything physical.

This motivation also works for children at school. For example, Cody and I visited the T. H. Rogers School in Houston, which taught special education to the most challenging of the learning-challenged children.

Jan asked if we'd be interested in working there: "They need a special dog, so I told them that we had the one for them."

I didn't hesitate. "We'll do it."

Cody had a special touch with kids, which might have come from his neighborhood walks. And even though he was really in his own element around children, this project wasn't going to be so simple, judging from the greeting that we got the first day. There were six children between the ages of six and nine, and most of them were clearly afraid of him. A couple of them even cried when they saw him. But Cody didn't flinch, and that helped all of us adults get into the right frame of mind, too.

Special education teachers are pretty special themselves. At T. H. Rogers, the teachers welcomed Dakota, perhaps for the same reason that physical therapists welcomed him: He gave them a bonus—help in motivating the kids, holding their attention, and keeping them focused on the task at hand. One of the things the teachers devised was a fun exercise to help the children learn to identify basic colors: We'd take Dakota behind a screen and place one of several different colored scarves into a backpack he wore. Then we'd bring Dakota back to the kids, and one of them would open the backpack and pull the scarf out.

"What color is this?" the teachers would ask the kids. The child who gave the correct answer would get to hug Dakota and give him a treat. The kids didn't answer correctly very often in those first weeks. But when the right answer did come out, the cause for celebration was so great that it almost verged on chaos.

A boy named Brett was the first one to get a color right without prompting, and he was so excited that he repeated it a dozen times: "Red, red, red, red . . ." He ran over and embraced Cody and gave him a treat, while the other kids cheered and repeated the color themselves.

The kids were rowdy and loud and strong, and they were difficult to control. Cody helped keep them in check. More than once, I saw a child standing there with a handful of Dakota's golden-reddish hairs, which had to have hurt him, but he didn't move and he never growled.

We went to the school twice a week for two hours a day, and sometimes it seemed it was as if each day there was our first. Sure, the kids remembered the dog, but the colors were still a mystery to them. These were long afternoons, filled with repetition of simple tasks, and the kids would wear out quickly. The teachers often gave them a break to lie down and rest, and Cody would join them. He kept his energy and focus with the children, and so did I. This became a personal project for me—I wanted those kids to be successful.

We practiced at home by taking every one of his toys out of the backpack, making noises, and jostling him, so he would be ready for anything. I soon realized that I was transferring the energy I'd previously used to worry about myself to getting ready for these visits each week.

"Let's go to school, Cody," was all it took to get him to the door. And then when we got there, he'd walk right to the classroom door without any direction from me. He loved these kids, and I believe that he knew he was helping them. Over the next few months, things started to happen: One by one, the kids started to get the colors right. When they realized that they were successful, their faces would light up with a sense of accomplishment. I could see their confidence growing and their social skills evolving. I wouldn't have traded anything for the look on those little faces when they got a color right and ran over to hug Dakota.

Soon, the teachers started putting letters of the alphabet into

Dakota's backpack, and we started spelling out the children's names. This was unbelievable to me. Once the kids knew they could learn with Dakota, they wanted more. I could see that the teachers were ecstatic to have made something happen for these children. And an important part of Dakota's role here as well was to help the teachers themselves find some reward and success in the very tough setting they faced every day.

Cody wore out after two hours, but the kids never wanted him to leave—they always begged him to stay and play some more. And even though I found the work tough but rewarding, I only had to face it twice a week. The kids' teachers—and their parents, too—had to go through it every single day.

To celebrate the progress we were making at T. H. Rogers, I got a huge red sack and filled it with teddy bears for each of the children at Christmas. Cody and I sat there, and each child came up for their bear. I made them tell me their name before they could get their bear, and they all were able to do that. The greatest Christmas gift I ever got was a collection of cards that these children had made for us—in their own handwriting.

At another school, Dakota regularly visited children with various disabilities. These kids were "mainstreamed" into the regular student body, but unfortunately that meant that they had to face harassment almost daily from some of their classmates. After those classmates found out that Dakota visited the disabled kids once a week, *they* wanted to become friends with him, too. Cody spent time with all of them, for he loved them all equally. Dogs don't see disabilities or differences, and I believe that his unconditional acceptance of kids who were different taught a lesson to the other children.

It didn't take many visits to the hospital and schools before I realized that I was getting another valuable lesson myself: I could manage my problems and live my life—now that I was choosing to do so. These children, however, were battling to live with their disabilities every single day. I saw a lot of kids who had little hope of ever leading a pain-free existence or a life without struggle. Yet, most of them could find a way to smile, especially when Cody came around. Whenever we showed up, the children all wanted to know what we were going to do that day. And they worked at whatever it was—seemingly watching Dakota for approval every step of the way, and sharing their accomplishments with him. This was a powerful thing to witness on an almost-daily basis.

■　　■　　■

We also visited a lot of seniors. This was a much different scenario than we saw with the children, of course. The responses that we received here ranged from sheer joy at Cody's company to therapeutic benefits from petting and hugging him.

The seniors all wanted to talk—sometimes they were melancholy, and sometimes they wanted to share happy memories. For instance, Cody reminded James of his own dog growing up; but for Sylvia, he was like her children's dog, which reminded her that they didn't visit her often enough.

"Does he like to swim?" Donald asked, thinking back to his hunting days. "Can he retrieve birds?"

"Sure, he's a great bird dog," I told him. As far as I knew, Cody had never been hunting a day in his life, but that didn't matter. The result was that my answer led Donald into a detailed discussion with me about bird dogs, birds, and hunting.

The important thing here wasn't so much what they were saying, but just that they were talking at all. Dakota helped bring them out, relax, and express their feelings, which a counselor couldn't always do. Many health-care professionals and administrators watched in wonderment as they heard some of their residents utter the first complete sentences they'd ever heard . . . and they said these sentences to a dog.

A lot of the seniors just hugged Cody, and they all had some little treat for him. Some of them had even made it a point to buy a box of dog biscuits to have on hand for his visits. They made room for him on the couch or in their beds. They spoke to him as if no one else was in the room. Some of them, who were suffering from various stages of dementia or Alzheimer's disease, were sure that he was *their* dog. "Please take good care of him for me. I miss him so," was something I heard more than once. I always promised these people that I'd take care of him as if he were my own.

One particularly hot and humid summer day, I first saw Dakota deal with death and dying. Annette was in her 90s, and even in the sweltering heat, her bed was covered with blankets, for she complained that she was cold and that she'd been unable to get warm for a long time. It was just her luck that I had a 98-pound bedwarmer with me. Cody gave her a sniff, and without any prompting from anyone, he gently climbed into bed with her. Since he was being so careful, I let him go, and he cuddled up right next to her.

Annette put her hand on him and smiled. I leaned in to hear her soft voice. "He's so warm," she said. "He feels good."

I smiled back and put my hand on her arm to show that I understood. Her expression and voice told me that she was at peace, that she knew that everything was okay now. She smiled one last time and closed her eyes. Within minutes, Annette was gone—Dakota had helped her reach her final resting place.

■　　■　　■

We did a lot of visiting on behalf of Paws for Caring. Since I didn't have to worry about a job, I had lots of time on my hands. I knew that the real star of our team was Dakota, and that I was only there to enable his visits. And I was honored to do so.

When Cody came into my life, I'd been in the process of getting ready to die. Things were different now. For example, in the summer of

1996, I was named Paws for Caring's Volunteer of the Year in the greater Houston area, thanks to Dakota. From the beginning, I knew that Jan and the people at Paws for Caring understood that I had a lot to gain from this activity, and they did everything they could to ensure that I was a beneficiary, too. It was really working for me. Dakota was the teacher and I was the student. He was teaching me to live for the moment, to enjoy each day as it came. I was starting to understand the golden-retriever outlook on life. He was teaching me about unconditional love, and that was the most powerful medicine I could get. And he was also filling my battle-scarred heart with joy every single day.

I had a new purpose in life, and I was happy and productive. It wasn't that long ago that I was trying to figure out how to end my life. Now I couldn't wait to get up each day and share my life with Dakota—and to share him with everyone who might need him. It was about this time that I began to realize that Cody was indeed a guardian angel, one who walked by my side every single day.

■ ■ ■ ■ ■

CHAPTER FIVE

The Gift

"Leave me alone!" I shouted to the small group that had gathered around me as I sprawled on the floor.

"Are you okay?" asked a female customer. "What can we do?"

My mind was racing: *Where am I? What am I doing here?* I'd already shoved a couple of nitroglycerin pills into my mouth, and I tried to speak more calmly to the concerned onlookers. "Just leave me alone—give my medication a chance to work."

I was having a severe angina attack, and it was just my luck that I happened to be in a very public place—the local WalMart. Usually Nancy helped me with the driving and kept an eye on me when I went out in public. This time, I was just trying to run a quick errand, and I hadn't given much thought to any possible heart episodes. So here I was, alone and having to worry about how everyone around me might over- or underreact, either of which could cause me problems. I was so happy with the way things were going with Dakota and my return to public life that I sometimes overlooked the fact that I was still burdened with the possibility of a health crisis at any time.

This was one of those times.

The heart is pretty independent and does just about anything it wants to do, good or bad. The good comes in the form of a long, healthy life. The bad is every time someone "just drops dead from a heart attack." Now, I have unstable angina, which isn't a heart attack—but they both start out the same way, and no matter what they call it, it still hurts . . . a lot. And it scares me—I live in fear every day that my next attack will be "the big one."

Meanwhile, back at WalMart, I survived, and most of the customers went back to their shopping. I unwound from the fetal position, took a few deep breaths, and sat up.

The store manager kneeled in front of me. "What do you need?" he asked. "Can we call someone?"

"I think I'll be okay in just a few more minutes. Sorry for creating a scene."

"That's the least of our concerns. I'm just glad that you're okay," he said. "I gather that you're used to dealing with this."

"Yes, I'm sorry to say I am." What I didn't share with him was that I was also feeling sorry for myself—for my vulnerability, for my loss of independence, and for the embarrassment I caused myself. Dakota was doing his job as a therapy dog, and my mental health was making a comeback—but a physical event like this one undid a lot of that psychological healing. It made me think about the fact that my life would never really get back to normal.

Being reminded of how close to death I was at any given moment could be really depressing and scary. I couldn't escape that fear. Cody or no Cody, I still occasionally backslid into thinking about using that gun I'd bought. After all, I still couldn't work, and I continued to have these attacks once or twice a week, often in an embarrassingly public way. Nancy and Jan saw to it that I stayed busy with Dakota and our AAT visits for Paws for Caring. That's what helped me fight back against the depression that unfortunately will always be there for me.

Working with kids was still the best prescription for my own well-being. There was a home and school for children with Down syndrome down the road from us. The kids went there for schooling and physical activities, ranging from walking to playing softball. Cody and I made this into a family event, with Nancy and Abbey joining us once a week throughout the summer. The children loved the dogs, and they helped motivate the kids to do a lot of different activities. It was great fun for Dakota and Abbey, too—after all, who plays ball better than a golden retriever?

I was still battling angina attacks. They could happen two or three times a day, or just once or twice a week. The doctors were trying to find the right drugs and the right dosages to help me control it, and over the first 18 months we were together, Cody witnessed hundreds of these painful episodes. He learned to crawl into bed with me or lie next to me on the floor, sometimes staying there for hours to help me fight through the attack. As my chest tied into a knot, I would squeeze him hard to shift my own pain. I know that he felt my pain, but he never flinched. There was nothing either of us could do, however, to keep these episodes from occurring.

One day in the fall of 1996, Dakota and I were visiting a school as part of Pet Awareness Week. Our veterinarian, Dr. Pat Choyce, had asked me to speak about animal-assisted therapy and service dogs. We were just starting our presentation when Cody started to act a little rambunctious. He was pawing at me and ignoring my instructions, acting as if he had a serious problem. I thought that maybe he was going to throw up or he needed to relieve himself. He'd never acted like this in public before, and, at the very least, I wanted to get him out of there to straighten him out. I was a little upset with him for making us leave in the middle of the program, but I apologized to our panel leader and took him off the stage.

I walked out the door of the auditorium, and just as the door closed behind me, I felt a crushing, sharp pain in my chest and a shortness of breath. My knees buckled and I blacked out. When I came to, there were a lot of people around me, yelling and screaming. I took my medication and sat there for a while collecting myself as the medication went to work. Dakota, who had never left my side, was licking my arms and my face.

Dr. Choyce was there, too, watching this amazing animal work on me. "Maybe he was trying to tell you something," he said.

"You may have something there," I told him.

I looked at Cody. His eyes seemed to be bluish-gray, a color I'd never seen before. A few minutes later, they were back to their normal brown. I decided that I was probably seeing this color change because I was still a little out of it.

Dr. Choyce drove me home, and we talked about this episode on the way. As I looked back over the past month or so, I could remember Dakota acting the same toward me each time I had an attack. At the time, however, I was blaming him for causing them. Maybe I should have been paying closer attention to him. I talked to Nancy about it when I got home, and she pointed out that just a couple of days before, Cody had pawed at me and had gotten very agitated while I was lying on the couch. I told him to leave me alone, but he wouldn't let up. Minutes later, I had an attack. In my mind, I blamed him for making me mad enough to push me into a medical emergency.

Now, I like to think that I'm a pretty smart person: I'm an engineer, I'm well educated, and I hold something like 17 patents. Yet I was reluctant to give Dakota credit for this ability because I just didn't think it was possible. But in my heart (so to speak), it slowly dawned on me that somehow Dakota was sensing when these attacks were about to occur.

I was at home the next time Cody exhibited this behavior. I was sitting at my desk, working at the computer, while he napped on the carpet. Suddenly, he transformed from a well-behaved, docile golden retriever into the medical caregiver from hell. Catching me completely by surprise, he nuzzled me and pushed his head up under my arm and into my leg. I got a little perturbed as he made me spill my cup of coffee all over my desk. Since I was now paying more attention to the coffee than to him, he pawed at me, put his paw first on my arm and then my leg, and gave me a little push, as if to say, "Hey! I'm not kidding!"

Finally, I realized what he was trying to tell me. Cody was trying to save my life. I could die in the next few minutes—the coffee could wait. If I was right about Dakota, if somehow he'd learned to sense when I was about to have an angina attack, then I figured that I ought to be able to do something with that warning. I took him seriously and I swallowed my medication immediately. And sure enough, an angina attack followed. Since I felt this one coming quickly, I headed directly for my bed.

Cody didn't relax, which led me to believe that this attack was going to be a bad one. I began to get hot and started to sweat. I felt short of breath, and my heart was trying to pound its way out of my chest. I was helpless. I tried to cry out for Nancy, but I wasn't sure where she was, and Dakota wouldn't leave my side to go get her.

Clearly I wasn't in control—this dog was. He completely took charge, climbing up on my bed and looking me in the eye to reassure me that he was here. Then he turned one of those dog circles and laid down in front of me, putting his back against my chest, as if to say, "Here you go, hang on." I gave him a quick hug and said a little prayer: "Please God, let this one be short."

God had other plans. The pain suddenly crushed me, twisting my chest into a knot as it shot through my entire body. This was a feeling I'd come to know. Normally, when an attack struck me without any warning, it would knock me to the ground. But this time, thanks to Dakota, I was ready to deal with it. Even with that advance warning, the pain quickly drained my strength, and I had to work hard to concentrate so that the medication would take effect quickly.

I felt Cody's warm body against mine, and I grabbed ahold of him. In spite of the growing pain and my increasing heart rate, I sensed his steady breathing. By emulating his calm presence and synchronizing my breathing with his, I was able to control my respiration rate and keep from hyperventilating. But the pain got worse, and my bear-hugging pressure on Dakota increased. He seemed to understand and, as he had many times before, he stayed with me without showing any sign of the pain that I know I was causing him. The time passed, and my anguish became more bearable. Little by little, the weight was lifted from my chest, I could breathe without pain, and my heart rate returned to something resembling normal.

Throughout this entire ordeal, Cody didn't move or even make a sound. As my grip on him lessened, he turned and sympathetically began to lick my hands, arms, and face. This told me that I'd survived. I rested for a few hours to regain my strength. Some of my attacks can be more serious than others, but having a warning clearly helped. The episode was much less severe than usual, and a head start on my medication helped counteract the attack and lessen its effects, while also avoiding an accident or a fall.

How did Cody know? He was exhibiting classic "alerting" behavior, typical of seizure-alert dogs—pawing at, nuzzling, or jumping on the ill person. Some service dogs have been doing this for years, alerting their human partners about an imminent medical event, such as an epileptic seizure or diabetic emergency. I'd heard about this from some other people with service dogs—they told amazing stories of how their dogs would "alert on" them in a crisis. So I understood the principles and knew the terminology, but in all of my reading and work with doctors and service-dog owners, I hadn't heard or read about a dog alerting on someone with heart problems.

Questions filled my mind: What did Cody smell, sense, or hear? What was he thinking? How did he come to learn this behavior? What was it that finally got him to recognize what was happening to me? How did he make the leap to realizing that he could help me? And most important—did he *know* that he was saving my life? Because that's exactly what he was doing by helping me get the medication into my system in advance, just like all those seizure-alert dogs did with their people. And the support he was giving me by absorbing my crushing hugs and helping me breathe was a very big part of it as well.

On this day, Dakota gave me my freedom back.

I'd been living—and nearly dying—with these angina attacks for close to five years. I thought back on that time frame, and about all of those scary, unpredictable episodes I'd had, such as the one in WalMart. I was vulnerable and dependent on other people to help me live my life, and I had to be careful about going out in public. But maybe I could begin to look at things differently.

Now that I knew what to look for, I almost wanted to have another attack soon so I could test this theory and see if Dakota would respond the same way again. You know what they say about being careful what you wish for: Two days later I was sitting in my recliner reading the paper when that big red furry paw came crashing through the sports page.

"Cody!" I snapped.

He took another swipe at me with that same paw. I didn't need to be told again. I took my pills and headed for the bedroom, literally hoping that I was about to have another attack. And I did. I had this very strange mix of pain and elation—I was hurting physically, of course, but it didn't seem quite as bad as it usually did. The medication was already at work. But something else was going on. I now had an alarm system for these attacks. A four-legged, 98-pound, reddish-gold alarm system. He was taking the job away from Nancy and others. Our lives were changing once again, thanks to Dakota.

■　　■　　■

There are a number of concepts regarding the ability of dogs to alert their human partners about different medical events, but very little supportive research. Dr. Rupert Sheldrake put forth three theories for these alerting behaviors in his book *Dogs That Know When Their Owners Are Coming Home: And Other Unexplained Powers of Animals: An Investigation.* The three theories are:

1. The animal notices subtle changes in behavior or muscle tremors of which the person is unaware.

2. The animal senses electrical disturbances within the nervous system associated with an impending seizure.

3. The animal smells a distinctive odor given off by the person before an attack.

Dogs are actually being trained to warn people about epileptic seizures and diabetic attacks in the United States and the United Kingdom. The training seems to be somewhat inexact and is based on teaching the dogs to react to certain smells or behavior in their human partner. According to Canine Partners for Life, the training for a seizure dog actually consists of reinforcing instinctive behavior, which is most likely a factor related to the dog's personality. And, in fact, a study at the University of Florida, reported on the Vetcentric Website [**www.vet-centric.com**], cited two factors as consistent in dogs with alerting behavior: a close bond with their human partner and an "alert" (but not frantic) disposition.

There's no known research on alerting behavior by dogs for angina or heart attacks, and apparently no training programs exist that are specific to heart issues. The popular theory among dog trainers and some medical doctors is that dogs smell an enzyme that the heart sends out in the beginning stages of the attack. That enzyme signals the brain to send more adrenaline into the system and to open the veins in response. One heart doctor told me that he thought that Dakota could actually smell my body's stress—probably in certain hormones or chemicals appearing in my body's perspiration—before I could even sense it.

Any of these concepts could have been connected to Cody and how he behaved when I had my attacks. He spent virtually every waking moment with me and came to know me and my body quite well.

It wouldn't have surprised me to discover that he could sense my increasing heart rate or smell the hormones springing into action.

No one taught Dakota this behavior—he learned it himself. And I, of course, had no idea that he could ever do such a thing. I had no idea that *any* dog could do this, and apparently neither did any of my health-care people. Dakota watched me suffer through hundreds of these angina attacks from the time he came to be with me, and I think that he just finally put everything together. Maybe he smelled something different about me, or maybe he just sensed that something was off. But in any case, he was able to make the connection between that and my subsequent painful response. I believe that he wanted to make sure that I was ready for what was coming next.

Susan Duncan, my mentor from Delta Society, was quoted in the piece I read on the Vetcentric Website. She spoke of the role of the seizure-alert dog—all things that I'd seen in Dakota. "The dog becomes a constant that can be relied upon, regardless of where a person is or whether other people are available to be with the person," she said. It seems that physically, the dogs could also help ensure the safety of their partners during a seizure, first by helping them sit or lie down, and then by discouraging unnecessary interference from people who aren't sure how to respond. "The calm presence of the dog can assure others that the person's seizure is not an unexpected event." And, she added, that calm presence is also important to the person as comforting " . . . to see the familiar dog after the seizure has taken place."

I called Susan to tell her what Dakota had done. "Mike, you've got yourself a service dog," she told me. "And since he's crucial to your well-being, he can and should go anywhere and everywhere with you."

I headed right to Delta Society's Website. It told me that federal civil rights law, specifically the Americans with Disabilities Act (ADA), defines a service animal as "any animal individually trained to do work or perform tasks for the benefit of a person with a disability." According to the ADA, a disability is "any physical or mental impairment that substantially limits a major life activity, such as caring for one's self, performing manual tasks, walking, seeing, hearing, speaking, breathing, learning, and working."

I learned that federal laws protect the rights of individuals with disabilities to be accompanied by their service animals in public places. To be protected by federal law, and to have the right of access with the animal to public areas otherwise closed to animals, the person must meet the definition of having a disability, and the animal must meet the definition of service animal. There was no doubt about it: Cody was now a service animal. My life depended on him, and I wasn't going anywhere without him.

We'd come a long way since that first night with the green rubber frog.

■　　■　　▇　　■　　■

CHAPTER SIX

The Teaching Begins

The way my life has gone, I know that every sunrise I see is a bonus. That's why I start each day the same way: "Thank you, God." And a certain four-legged, red-haired angel always comes next: "Thank you, Dakota."

I probably should have been buried by now, written up as a chapter in a medical textbook. I was going to kill myself, or my heart was going to do it for me. But then, this wonderful golden retriever with a special gift came along to keep me alive. More than that, he gave me a reason to live. It's because of him that I've had the chance to greet so many sunrises.

When I go out in public, it isn't obvious that I have heart problems, but according to the definitions of the Americans with Disabilities Act (ADA), I *do* have a disability. Even though it's an invisible one, it still allows me to have a trained service dog with me anywhere and everywhere I go. There are other "invisible" or "hidden" disabilities—epilepsy, lung disease, diabetes, psychological or emotional disorders, and hearing and vision impairments all fall under that definition. People with those disabilities also have the right to have a service dog with them at all times. The laws are very precise guaranteeing that right.

However, they're not so precise in other ways—for instance, there's no requirement for someone with a disability to answer questions regarding their handicap, nor is there any standard identification badge or card or required equipment for either the human or the dog.

People are accustomed to seeing Labrador retrievers and golden retrievers or German shepherds doing the work of service dogs, but they can be any breed or mixed breed of any size or age. Many service dogs are trained by their human partners to deal with their very specific disabilities, and consequently, there are no national requirements or standards to define a service dog. That's why the laws are written the way they are—to protect people with disabilities and to allow them to participate in a dignified and nonconfrontational manner in any life activity.

Dignity was the key word for me. I was both excited and apprehensive about the opportunity to go back out in public with my service dog. But it required that I admit—continually and in a very obvious way—that I have a disability. Embracing my handicap was a big first step, for I had to show my pain in public and admit that I have an imperfection. It wasn't going to be easy, but I was ready to give it a shot.

■   ■   ■

I found out very quickly that there were a lot of shop owners, restaurant managers, taxi drivers, grocery store clerks, security personnel, and others who didn't understand: They didn't understand the law, they didn't understand our special challenges, they didn't understand our history, and they didn't understand the reality of what those with disabilities have to go through every day of our lives—the courage that it takes to step out into public, with or without a service dog. But it was the worst when people were just plain intolerant and didn't want to deal with something outside of their circle of comprehension.

I had a pretty good understanding of my rights with a service dog, and I guess I was a little naïve when I first set out to do more with Dakota by my side. But the reality was that I had many problems when I starting taking him out in public.

One of the first places I ventured into was a large discount department store. I was halfway down the first aisle when an employee came up to me. "I'm sorry, sir," she said. "We don't allow dogs in here."

"This is a service dog," I told her.

"Well, we allow guide dogs, but you're not blind, are you?"

"No, I'm not, but this is my service dog, and the law says that I can have him with me."

"I'm sorry, sir, I'll have to ask you to leave. That's our rule."

"Is there a manager here I can talk to?"

She pointed over my shoulder. "Here he comes right now."

"Hello, sir," he said. "Is there a problem here?" I could tell by his voice that he was going to be just as polite and uninformed as his clerk was, but I gave it a try anyway.

"I was just explaining to her what the law says regarding accessibility for my service dog," I replied. I was trying to stay calm and polite myself, but I could feel other customers looking at us. *Dignity*—I kept coming back to that word.

"We allow guide dogs in the store, but that's it," he said. This was my first confrontation, and I was beginning to waver a little. *I don't really know how far to take this,* I thought. *Maybe I'll just come back some other time.*

"I think you're making a mistake," I told him. "You should read the ADA laws, because you're actually risking a big fine and some legal trouble."

"I'm sorry, sir, but those are our rules. You're welcome in the store, but you'll have to leave your dog in the car."

It wasn't worth fighting at this point. I was still a little new at this, so I promised myself that I'd be back some other day when I was better prepared to do battle.

Variations of this kind of exchange took place many times over the next few months as Cody and I ventured out more. For the first time in my life, I was feeling the sting of prejudice and discrimination. This had never happened to me before. I had to keep track of where we were allowed and where we weren't. I was growing weary of the confrontations, and it was easier for me to just avoid certain places.

But one day, as we were in another losing discussion with another building manager as to what our rights were, I looked into Dakota's eyes. I knew that we weren't going to take it anymore. We had every right to be there, and we should be able to enjoy those rights without having to plead our case to get them.

Dignity.

During this time, I had several conversations with Susan Duncan, director of the National Service Dog Center at Delta Society. She was very supportive of us, and told me how to deal with these situations and exactly what our legal rights were. She fielded a lot of calls from me, and we became very good friends. I got to the point where I was ready to go to battle for Dakota and me, and for anyone else with a disability and a service dog. I carried copies of the ADA laws and worked hard to educate anyone who questioned our right to be anywhere. With Susan's support, I went through Delta's ADA training program and became certified to teach ADA compliance. Susan helped me get involved in a network of other people with service dogs.

Cody and I never looked back, and never took no for an answer again. That list I was keeping of where we hadn't been allowed? Well, that became my assignment sheet of places to revisit. I didn't want to be confrontational—I really did want to educate these people and their institutions. And, once I became more proficient at presenting the facts, most of them ended up being quite gracious. But if they didn't want to listen and learn, I'd invite the local police to come and help me.

I was finally ready to go back to the department store where I'd had my first discriminatory experience. It was a busy Saturday morning—but apparently it wasn't busy enough to keep Mr. Polite-but-Uninformed from spotting me. He caught up to me within minutes.

"Sir, I'm sorry, but I thought we had an understanding that your dog wasn't allowed in here," he said.

"Well, we actually never had 'an understanding,' because I knew that you were mistaken and in violation of federal law." I admit that I'd rehearsed that line a few times in my head. As I handed him a copy of the ADA laws, I said, "Here's some information for you about the law you're breaking."

He barely looked down at it. "I'll have to ask you to leave."

"I'm sorry, but I'm not going to leave this time." I wished I hadn't gone so meekly the first time.

"Sir, I hope you aren't going to make me call the police."

"Well, if that's what it takes, go right ahead," I told him. "And I hope that you don't mind if *I* make some calls, too. I have some other friends with service dogs who would be very interested in coming here to hear your response, too. And if you're certain that you're doing the right thing, then I know you won't mind if I call the newspapers and TV stations to see if they want to come over and help you tell your rules to their readers and viewers as well."

By this time, several customers and a couple of employees had gathered around us and were watching the scene unfold. The manager looked around—if he was bluffing, he'd just blinked.

I took the opening and kept rolling. "The police will just come in here and create a scene while they explain the law to you. I'd rather that you let *me* explain it, to save us both a lot of time and trouble."

He glanced down and looked at the brochure that I'd given him, which had a particular section highlighted.

"Take a look at this," I said, pointing to the highlighted area. "This sentence right here says it all."

Service animals are provided for under the Code of Federal Regulations (CFR) Part 36, 36.104, and 36.302. The American with Disabilities Act guarantees a blind, deaf, or physically disabled person the right to be accompanied by a service animal in all areas open to the general public. Service animals means any guide dog, signal dog, or other animal individually trained to do work or perform tasks for the benefit of an individual with a disability.

He read quietly. "Okay, you can stay for now. But I'll have to call my home office to see how they want me to handle it in the future," he said, trying to keep some control.

We'd begun to turn the tide. "I know what they're going to tell you, because they'll know the law. I'll guarantee that." I had him right where I wanted him, and now it was time to close. "How about if I come back sometime and teach a class to you and your employees about the ADA and the rights of service-dog access? It will keep you and your company out of a lot of trouble and make life better for people like me, who have disabilities but want to be your customers."

He gave me a half smile—the first sincere one I'd seen from him yet. "All right, why don't you call me and we'll talk." He handed me his business card and looked down at Dakota for the first time. "Can I pet him?"

How about that? He knew the etiquette about asking to pet a working service dog, but he didn't know the law about allowing them into his place of business. I could tell that he was probably a good man at heart, but he was just caught up in corporate politics and trying to do what he thought he was supposed to do for his employer.

And so it went—one business and building at a time. In our travels, we even ran into an occasional police officer who didn't fully understand the law, and we welcomed the chance to educate them, too. Soon, Dakota and I could go anywhere in town and do anything that anyone else could do, without being questioned. This gave me a new sense of self-reliance and self-worth.

I owed not only my life, but the ability to enjoy a normal and fulfilling lifestyle, to Cody and the ADA. I knew the ADA laws: I realized that I didn't have to tell people about my disability or what my dog did for me; I knew that I didn't have to make him wear anything special to identify him as a service dog; and I understood the confusion the general public had about the ADA and the role of service animals covered by the law.

I always felt that most people were good by nature and if they were given the chance to understand why I needed Dakota, they'd accept us. So I took another step to help educate them: I ordered a red vest from Delta Society and had it embroidered with the words "Service Dog." This vest plainly said that Cody was a very special dog and that he was my partner—he was allowed to go anywhere that I could.

The vest worked. It opened doors, but more important, it opened up avenues of communication with people in the general public. They often asked first if they could pet him, and then they'd ask me some general questions about service dogs. Sometimes the questions went beyond the letter of the law or where I might have let them go if they were a business owner or a building manager. But I welcomed the opportunity to educate one more person. And I was incredibly proud to be making a difference.

But just as important to me was what we'd accomplished for those who followed us into those public places with their own service dogs. If someone had already challenged me, then they wouldn't be bothering the little girl with her epileptic-seizure-alert dog or the person with a mobility-assistance dog. Even today, I feel that I have to teach what I know to others. I won't rest until everyone understands these rights, including those people in the public sector who control access for service dogs.

This started simply as a way to assert my right to have my lifesaving companion with me wherever I go, but it's become a larger life lesson now. We've broken down barriers of ignorance and discrimination for people with disabilities, and we've actively taught tolerance and acceptance.

Some good is coming from the pain and suffering that I've endured, as I've been handed the opportunity to give something back to society. I was excited about the fact that, for the first time in a number of years, I clearly had a mission, a calling in life . . . and a reason to go on living.

※　※　※　※　※

Back to the Real World

Dakota's newfound alerting talent was saving my life and giving Nancy's back to her. Now that she knew that Dakota's eyes and nose were taking care of me, my wife's load had been lightened considerably. Of course she still watched me, but she didn't have to live every moment with me and for me, like she once did. That was a good thing, because now her father, Harold, needed her help. It was 1998, and Harold was quite elderly and starting to have some serious health issues. Nancy was really worried about him.

Harold was a widower, and he lived by himself in Duncansville, Pennsylvania. So we loaded Dakota and Abbey into Nancy's Jeep and hit the road to visit him. With two big dogs, we'd gotten into the habit of driving most places, rather than leaving Abbey behind or putting her into airline cargo while Cody got to ride in the cabin. So we put a comforter over the suitcases in the back of the Jeep, and that's where Cody traveled. He loved the view from there and had plenty of room to stretch out. Abbey got the backseat all to herself.

There were no surprises for us in Pennsylvania—it was evident that Harold needed some help. So Nancy and I discussed it on the drive home.

"His house needs some work, but we could live in the basement while we do some repairs on the rest of the place," she said.

I agreed with her. "There's nothing keeping us in Houston. And I actually wouldn't mind getting back to Pennsylvania." Nancy and I are both Pennsylvania natives; in fact, we met in high school and attended college there. Moving back wasn't that tough of a decision, so we decided to get home, put the house up for sale, and start packing.

I was behind the wheel as we hit the state of Louisiana. I could always tell when I got to Louisiana because it would be raining—and usually it would be raining hard. This day was no exception. The rain was coming down in sheets, which made the windshield wipers useless. As we drove onto one of the causeways, it got really torrential, and we had to dodge the other vehicles on the road. These causeways always got my full attention because they have no shoulders or exits—there's just the occasional turnout. I hugged the right lane, probably doing about 40 miles an hour. The big trucks, of course, were flying by us as if we were standing still, throwing water all over us and blowing us all over the place.

I was working hard to stay in control when suddenly Dakota was in my face. *Geez,* I thought, *we just made a potty stop a few miles back. Does he really have to go again?*

"Go on, Cody. You're just going to have to wait a bit," I told him. On these causeways, there was nowhere to pull off, not even to the side of the road. But Dakota didn't seem to care. He just kept pushing at me. "Nancy, can you do something about him?" I asked. "I've kind of got my hands full over here."

"Dakota, get back there," Nancy said. But he was having nothing of it. "Are you sure that he's not sick? Maybe he has to throw up or something," she said.

That big red paw took a full swing at me. Simultaneously, Nancy and I realized what was going on: an alert. Suddenly—miraculously— a turnout appeared out of nowhere on the side of the road. I was already feeling an attack coming on as I pulled over and threw the gearshift into "Park." The Jeep was still rocking as Nancy handed me my medication. Through the pain, I held on to the steering wheel with all my strength and fought my way through another of these episodes I had come to know so well.

It was one thing to have an attack at home or even in a public place, for there was no danger to anyone else. But on the causeway, the situation could have turned tragic. If it had happened 20 seconds earlier or 20 seconds later, or if Dakota hadn't alerted on me in time, I would have been past that pullout and in the throes of a medical emergency in traffic in a driving rainstorm. A lot of people could have been hurt or killed.

Dakota had saved my life twice that day—once by alerting on me and allowing me to get my medicine, and again by getting me out of traffic. He also saved Nancy's, Abbey's, and his own life, and who knows how many others. We sat there for a while, pondering those things.

"Are you okay?" Nancy asked me. "I love you."

"I love you too, Nancy."

I had survived another attack. We said a little prayer, then headed back to Houston with Nancy driving. The rain had let up, and hopefully our adventure was over. Dakota stayed in the backseat with Abbey, leaning into the front to lick my face and arms, which was his normal routine after I've suffered an attack. I petted him and said, "And I love you, too, Cody."

■　　■　　■

Although it was difficult for Nancy and me to see my father-in-law's health deteriorating, it was nice being back in Pennsylvania. I certainly didn't miss Houston's humidity or smog. At least now I was able to breathe comfortably again.

We spent a lot of time fixing up Harold's house. He'd lived there for such a long time that a lot of work needed to be done, both on the house and on his possessions. The work kept Nancy and me very busy, but one of the first things I did when we got there was buy a fishing boat. Nancy didn't care for fishing, so this became a special time for Dakota and me. We both enjoyed the drive over to Lake Raystown— we'd watch the countryside and look for cows in the heart of Pennsylvania dairy country. When we got to the lake, Cody would help me put the boat in the water by keeping an eye on me to be sure I was safe. Plus, it gave him an excuse to step into the water.

Many days it didn't even matter if I had bait on the hook or not— we just enjoyed each other and our quiet time together. If I did get a fish, Dakota got really excited and wanted to help take it off the hook. We swam together, too, and I'd watch this beautiful creature just glide in the water, free to enjoy his place and time here on Earth. We'd listen to the birds and other wild animals and enjoy the tranquility of the world around us, free from pain and anger.

I treasured this time, and I believe that Cody did, too. When darkness would fall, I realized that I'd made it through another day, with Dakota there to keep me safe. On the quiet ride home, his head would be on my lap, and I could feel his warmth. All was well. I'd reach up and touch the little gold angel that was pinned to the sun visor of the Jeep, and then I'd rub Cody's head. I looked forward to many more days together.

But for as much as these outings meant to me, there was still something inside of me that cried out to go back to work. Nancy and I talked about it, and she was totally supportive. To tell the truth, she'd probably had enough of my being home every day. I didn't really have a specific plan—after all, it had been six years since my heart attacks and open-heart surgery. I wasn't quite sure where to start to look for a job, but I did get a number of calls each week from former colleagues, who gave me updates on the projects they were working on and all the people we knew. But even though I spoke to my former co-workers regularly, I was afraid that no one really missed me. I felt like damaged goods.

One particular engineer friend and I spoke on a semiweekly basis, just to visit and stay in touch. One day I mentioned to him that I thought I was ready to go back to work, for I felt that having Dakota there to protect me would allow me to return to engineering.

A few days later, the phone rang, and a familiar voice at the other end said, "I understand you're looking for work." It was Dick Tansill, a senior vice president for my old company, Parsons Transportation Group.

I grinned. "Dick, how are you doing?"

"I'm great, but more important, how are *you* doing?"

"I'm getting better every day. I think I'm ready to take another shot at this work thing that I've heard so much about."

He laughed. "Can you come to Pittsburgh? We're in the middle of this light rail project here, and I need some help with the communications system." That was my specialty. If I was going to have a chance to be successful, it was exactly the kind of project I needed to come back to.

"I'm your guy," I told him. "The only thing is, I come with a partner. You won't have to pay him much, but he's going to be with me every step of the way."

"I've heard all about Dakota," Dick said. "I knew he was part of the deal, and we want him, too." I don't really remember the rest of the conversation. I couldn't tell Nancy any details about salary or benefits when she asked. I just knew that I was going back to work. I didn't tell Dick, but I would have worked for free.

I did have to give some thought to the logistics of this undertaking, however. The Parsons office in Pittsburgh was about a two-and-a-half-hour drive from Duncansville. I decided that I'd go up the night before I started and spend the rest of the week up there in a hotel. I didn't want to burn myself out with the commute—I knew that I'd need all my energy back on the job.

It didn't seem like that day would ever come. I felt like a little kid heading off to the first day of school—I had my bags packed, my brief-case loaded, a fresh battery for my laptop, my pencils sharpened, a bag for Dakota . . . I couldn't have been any more ready than I was. Or so I thought. I'd been thinking about a lot of things ever since Dick asked me to come back to work. But in the context of hanging out at the house and taking care of the day-to-day details of our lives, I didn't really have the chance to give the job my full attention until I got behind the wheel and headed down the highway toward Pittsburgh.

A complete range of fears and doubts clouded my mind. As I drove, I kept talking to Dakota: "It's been six years since my heart attacks and surgeries took me away. What's happened since then? I've tried to keep up with some basic computer technology, but e-mails and JPEG photos are a long way from the technical-engineering protocols and schematics that I need to know. What's gone on in the industry since 1992? Technology has been changing at lightning speed, especially in my field. How fast can I pick it up?"

And quite simply, I worried about my brain. It had shut down for a few hours while I was on life support during those surgeries, and a lot of stuff simply went away. I remembered how I had to relearn some very basic things about my world, like my grandkids' names and how to write. Those things all came back to me eventually, but what else fell into that heart-attack-caused abyss in my brain? Was I going to be smart enough to keep up? Would I still have the competitive edge so crucial for success in this field? And what about Dakota? Would he thrive in an office environment? Would he still be able to alert on me? Would others in the office welcome him?

I didn't want to be a burden to Parsons, to Dick Tansill, or to any of our clients. I'd been a constant encumbrance for someone or something for the past six years. Now, thanks to a lot of hard work, a little luck, and God's will, I felt that I was now beyond that point in my personal life. But I needed to take the next step. I needed to prove to myself that I could get back my professional life. Yet I didn't want to be some token guy for the Americans with Disabilities Act. I wanted to make a meaningful contribution. This wasn't child's play. My pride would still drive me to want to be the best, like I was before. Could I do that? Could I live up to my own expectations? Could I be the guy I remembered, the engineer that Dick Tansill remembered? Could I be the man in the workplace that I wanted to be?

It was a little ironic that Cody could keep me alive, but he couldn't help me at work. He wasn't able to show me where to put the numbers in my Excel spreadsheet, nor could he make my calculator function. After spending the past six years learning how to depend on Dakota for everything, I was more or less on my own now. But, as I looked over at Dakota in the passenger seat, he was sitting up, looking at me as if he was hearing my every thought. Those unbelievable eyes of his were looking straight at me—straight *through* me, really. And they were that bluish-gray color I'd seen that day at school. Just like that, I had my answer. I was still scared, but I knew that Dakota was with me.

The drive took forever. By the time I got to the hotel, I'd pretty much addressed all the psychological issues I was facing, and I was drained. I didn't have many answers, but at least I had a pretty good idea of what all the questions would be.

That night I took a huge step: It was my first time in years being away from Nancy, but I was taking that step with Cody, for I was now under his supervision and care. From that moment on, *every* step I took would be with him, and I was happy about that. We went out for dinner that night, and through all the apprehension and questions, I began to feel some newfound pride. I started having more pleasant thoughts than the worries I'd had on the drive: *I'm going back to work. I'll be the breadwinner once again. I'm going to build communication systems. And I'll be back with my guys.*

I didn't sleep much that night, as many things just kept rattling through my brain. And when I didn't sleep, neither did Dakota. I held on to him and talked to him throughout the night. His quiet strength comforted me, and I think that helped me finally fall asleep for a few hours.

At 8 o'clock the next morning, we went marching in the front door at Parsons.

The security guard was ready for us. "Good morning, Mr. Lingenfelter. And good morning, Dakota."

Dick Tansill had already made some special arrangements for us. First, obviously, he'd told the building staff to welcome us appropriately. Up until now, this had strictly been a "No Animals Allowed" facility. But we were an immediate exception, and no one asked us any embarrassing questions or challenged to our right to be there. Second, Dick had alerted the paramedics that we were going to be working in the building so that they could be aware of our presence, my special needs, and of Dakota's role in my health care. And finally, he informed the staff that I was going to be there with my service dog. Dick told me that only one person had objected, but he'd informed them that Dakota was here to stay, and if that person wanted to be, too, they'd need to adjust their attitude. (Actually, a few weeks later, after falling in love with Dakota, that person identified himself to me and apologized for prejudging.)

We didn't really do much that first day, other than meeting with everyone and getting up to speed on a few issues. Even though he'd turned me over to other people for most of these chores, I know that Dick kept a good eye on me the entire time.

We were accepted without question. Everyone enjoyed meeting Cody, and he was a big hit . . . as always. I was so happy to be back at work, and I think Dakota felt that from me. I think he was happy to be there by my side—but that part never changed, whether we were in an office building in Pittsburgh or on our fishing boat on Lake Raystown.

By the time we got back to the hotel, we were exhausted. We ordered some room service, and had absolutely no problem getting to sleep that night.

Over the next few months, I was amazed at how fast everything came back to me, and how quickly I picked up new procedures and information. Dakota and I were assimilated into the office's flow as if we'd been there forever. One of the engineers referred to Dakota as my "nonintrusive shadow." I was glad to have him there, and happy that he fit in so well at the office. It was a wonderful, challenging time, and I felt like I was productive and whole again. I started out working a few days each week in the office and the rest of the week at home. But by the end of the project, I was there five days a week.

Dakota seemed to enjoy our new routine. He loved chasing the pigeons in the city parks, and the week before Christmas, he was particularly excited about making the acquaintance of a policeman's horse. What made it all the more exciting was the fact that the horse was wearing fake reindeer antlers. Dakota's playful posturing with whatever animal he imagined this to be drew several spectators and made a lot of people smile.

But we hit a few snags along the way. Sure, the weekly commute was a pain, but the toughest part was being away from Nancy all week. We also had to put our animal-assisted therapy and ADA activities on hold while we got back into the work routine, and we missed that. But Nancy and I knew that we'd eventually get back into it because it meant so much to us.

And at work, there was one project manager who didn't seem to like me. I don't know why, but we just didn't hit it off, and he seemed to relish a confrontation with me every so often. While I didn't really enjoy it, I was never one to back down. But Cody had enough of it. During one of those blowups, he got up from the floor and started poking at me. He pulled me by my shirtsleeve and took me away from the situation. He didn't seem to be in the same behavior as his alerts, but I took my medication anyway. As it turns out, it wasn't an alert—it was just Dakota's way of getting me out of a stressful situation.

This project manager would keep Dakota quite busy over the next few months. In fact, it got to the point where Cody's behavior would tell me when this guy was on his way to my office. And apparently, I wasn't his only verbal punching bag, as several members of the office staff would come in to pet Dakota to help them recover from their own dealings with that project manager.

By the spring of 1998, we were nearing completion of the job in Pittsburgh, and I was wondering what might be next. The Parsons people seemed happy with my work, and we were getting great results. I was ready for more.

At the time, Parsons was involved with a state-of-the-art project in Buffalo, called an Intelligent Transportation System (ITS). Television cameras and other monitoring devices were being installed on the highway system around the metropolitan area, along with information signs to keep the general public informed of road conditions and weather. This was a very advanced communication system—it was all digital and used the very latest equipment and software. Part of the project was an all-new control center that would become part of a statewide monitoring system.

Dick asked if I could help out there with some design work. It was another commute for me, but I had to go where the work was. After all, there wasn't too much going on in Duncansville. It was a challenging job in Buffalo, but we finished off the major part of the project fairly quickly. There would be follow-up work at some later date, but I was glad we were done because this commute (five and a half hours) was really starting to get to me.

Dick was certainly keeping me busy. He asked me if I'd be interested in a Parsons project in Dallas starting that fall—being responsible for the design and construction management of the communication system for the light-rail expansion of Dallas Area Rapid Transit (DART). This would be a big move for me, total responsibility for a project like this. It would mean that I was back for keeps, returning to where I once was. I felt that I was prepared for the challenge.

Nancy and I talked it over that night, and she was fully supportive. We knew that a commute wasn't going to work this time, so we decided that we'd move to Dallas and take her father with us. It meant a return to the Texas weather, but Dallas was a different place from Houston, farther inland and just as hot, but a little drier. Anyway, I figured that I could stand the weather in exchange for what this new position would mean for me. Dakota and I went there first and lived in a hotel so I could get started on the job, and after a few weeks, Nancy and her father joined us. After a weekend of house hunting, we bought a home in the suburb of Plano and settled into our new lives.

■　　■　　■　　■　　■

CHAPTER EIGHT
Believing in Dakota

W as I getting right back on the road that had led me so close to death before? Of course, working felt good to me . . . but it also felt pretty good back in 1992. I was feeling the need to make this work, to forsake everything else in my life for success on the job.

I wanted to believe that Dakota was here to help me stay off the workaholic road. But yet I felt this compulsion—the same one I'd felt back then—to work more and more hours and to achieve professional and personal perfection. Somehow I had to make up for all that lost time. I wanted to show the world that I'd beaten this heart thing, at least on the outside. But I wondered if I was doing the right thing. The truth was that I'd never expected my life to be this good again. I never thought I'd have to make any decisions like this, because I didn't think that anyone would be asking me to return to work.

But after six years, I was no longer a burden on my wife, my family, or society in general. I could sleep peacefully at night, knowing that Dakota was there for me. I was still battling my angina, but thanks to Cody's vigilance, I had enough forewarning of the attacks that I didn't have to endure embarrassing blackouts in public places—and I didn't suffer from suicidal depression anymore. I was happy and whole again, and I owed it all to my four-legged angel. But I still owed a lot to my family, too. Was I making the right choices for them, as well as for myself? It's true that Nancy had always been supportive of whatever I wanted to take on, but I owed it to her to really think about these things. Even though I felt ready to take this step, I couldn't do it without Nancy and Dakota taking it with me. And so, with their support, I headed off to Dallas.

The project I was involved in was based out of the Dallas Area Rapid Transit (DART) office in downtown Dallas. DART was a pretty progressive company, and they had no issues with Dakota. In fact, he fit right in, for DART was a public transportation company that worked very hard to accommodate disabled riders and their service dogs.

The people in the DART office knew all about Dakota's alerting abilities. If they hadn't seen it in person, they'd certainly heard about it, either from me or someone else who was there when it happened. There really seemed to be great respect for Cody in the office. Oh sure, they all loved the dog—who doesn't love a golden retriever?—but this was a little more than that.

On a normal day at the office, you could feel a certain amount of tension in the air. Our work was always under some kind of pressure as we tried to meet deadlines, get the best prices, bid a job correctly, deal with cost overruns and change orders, or get suppliers to perform delivery miracles. There were a lot of type-A folks in that office, and we yelled at each other a lot. Most of the time it wasn't personal or vicious, it was just loud. Although it was the reality of our business, it did create an atmosphere that could be difficult at times.

My cubicle was the home of one standing joke for the vice presidents and managers. As they headed into a meeting, they'd stop in to see Dakota. "What do you think, Dakota?" they'd ask. "Take a whiff—how do I smell? Can I go into this meeting or should I go home?" They said it jokingly, but most of us knew that there was some reality in what they were saying.

And just about everyone, at one time or another, took comfort in stopping by just to pet Dakota. This was one of the most basic principles of animal-assisted therapy, after all—petting a dog is good for you. It lowers the blood pressure and relaxes your mind and body. I firmly believe that every stressful workplace should have a resident four-legged therapist.

I was happy to share Cody with the office, but he was still working full time for me—which was a good thing, because those angina attacks kept coming on a fairly regular basis. A lot of them were more bothersome than threatening. The chest pains could be agonizing, but I could fight my way through them. Often, Dakota's role was simply to be there for me to squeeze during the attack and to hold when it was over. He was able to warn me about the major attacks by alerting on me, usually two to five minutes before I could feel them coming. If I was at the office, I had a small room that I could go into to ride out the attacks. The office personnel knew that they were to come and check on me if I wasn't back in a half hour. If I was at home for a major attack, I usually had enough warning from Dakota so I could take my pills, get into bed, and hang on to him until the pain had passed.

The major attacks were excruciating, but Dakota's alerts gave me a head start on getting the medication into my system, which probably prevented the episodes from moving to a major heart attack. And Cody was there for me to squeeze, to transfer my own pain and help regulate my breathing. I believe that he was saving my life every time he alerted on me. Perhaps he was just saving me some pain, but there was no doubt that he'd indeed saved my life on several occasions. And the amazing thing is that, outside of taking a short break once in a while at the office, I missed only a few days of work.

Just when I thought I couldn't be more impressed by Cody's abilities, he surprised me again. An engineer named Bill had his cubicle about 50 feet or so down the hall from mine. We often carpooled to work together, and since Bill and Cody were good buddies, Cody would sometimes wander over to say hello at various times during the day. I think Bill was sneaking him a biscuit now and then, even though he knew that Cody was supposed to be on a diet.

Anyway, I was on my way to a meeting one morning when I called to Dakota. I looked up to see that he wasn't there. Now I knew he wouldn't be too far away, as he never ventured beyond where he could smell or hear me. So I started out, figuring that he must have been making his rounds here in the cubicles, looking for biscuits and pats on the head. I found him with Bill, who was sitting in his chair trying to work. When I got there, Dakota didn't even look up at me—he was pawing away at Bill.

"Cody, I'm not giving you any more cookies. Go with Mike, leave me alone." Bill was chuckling at the situation, but I knew exactly what was going on, and it was no laughing matter.

"Bill, Dakota's alerting on you," I said.

"What?"

"He's alerting on you," I repeated, aware that Bill had a history of heart problems. "Do you feel okay?"

"Mike, I feel fine, but I'll tell you one thing: If Dakota says I'm going to have a heart attack, let's get to the doctor." Bill had seen Dakota in action enough to trust him. He didn't have a heart doctor, so I called my cardiologist, Dr. Gene Henderson.

"Gene, Cody just hit on a guy here at work," I said. "He needs help right now. Can I bring him over?"

Dr. Henderson asked if Bill was in pain.

"Not yet," I told him. "But he does have a history, so I convinced him—Cody convinced him, actually—that he better get to a doctor."

Dr. Henderson knew Cody, too, so he said, "Well, get him over here."

We got to Dr. Henderson's office fairly quickly, and Bill still wasn't showing any signs of trouble. He looked at me and said, "Maybe Dakota really did just want a cookie."

For his sake, I hoped that was the case, but I put my faith in Dakota every day. "Well, as long as we're here, let's see what we can find out," I said.

Dr. Henderson's nurse pulled Bill in right away. Cody and I sat in the waiting room, and about 15 minutes later, I sensed a little commotion in the office. One of the nurses came out to tell me that Bill had suffered a full cardiac arrest on the stress treadmill in the exam room. They had stabilized him, but he was being taken to the hospital. The next day, Bill had bypass surgery. When this news got back to the office, I was sure that it would increase the pre-stressful-meeting traffic through my cubicle every morning for checkups from Dakota. Whether or not the people in the office believed that Cody could see their heart difficulties, he certainly was the talk of the office.

But I was still his number-one customer. One June night in 1999, Dakota jumped into bed with me at 5 A.M. and exhibited alerting behavior, even though I was fast asleep. He persisted in this, which drew Nancy's attention. She tried to wake me, but didn't get a response, so she called 911 right away. As it turns out, I was having a full-blown heart attack in my sleep. My blood pressure had dropped to 60 over 38, and without Cody's alert, I would never have awakened that morning. My recollection of the event was understandably somewhat hazy, but Nancy told me that Cody stayed right there to comfort me, never moving from the bed.

I do have one very real, clear, and vivid memory of that morning. I couldn't move, but at one point I opened my eyes and saw Dakota looking right at me. In his blue-gray eyes were two gold angels. For all the comfort that he'd given me, for all the special time that we'd spent together, for all the conversations that we'd shared, this was the first time that I had seen anything like this. What did it mean? I took it as a sign that I was surrounded by a very special presence, that I was being watched over by some greater power, and that everything was going to be all right. I remember feeling warm all over, and I was reassured that I would survive this crisis.

And I did survive. I took a little time off from work, but I was soon back in the office. Dakota was once again a calming presence for everyone. He was a very real, lifesaving hero for many . . . but especially for me.

■　　■　　■

Cody and I started to get back into our work for animal-assisted therapy and the Americans with Disabilities Act (ADA). I was visiting schools from time to time, mostly to talk about service dogs and the rights of people with disabilities. I was asked to serve on the board of directors for Service Dog Companions of Texas, which opened up even more opportunities to get out in public and raise awareness of the ADA, and accessibility rights for service dogs. Dakota and I spent a lot of time in Dallas working with local business leaders, teaching about the ADA and the rights of people with disabilities.

It was about this time that Susan Duncan of Delta Society came to town for meetings on the organization's behalf. Because I'd told her all of these stories about Dakota, as well as about DART's commitment to ADA practices, she made it a point to visit DART one day to thank us for our efforts. This was the first time that I'd met Susan in person—although we'd spent so much time together on the telephone that she seemed like an old friend.

Susan is an attractive woman who's barely bigger than her service dog, Lincoln (another beautiful golden retriever). Susan may be petite, but her heart is huge, and so is her dedication to service dogs and their partners. She has great eyes, with a twinkle that tells you that she makes things happen. She's been challenged by multiple sclerosis for many years, but that just adds to her resolve and to her credibility as director of Delta's National Service Dog Center. If she were a general in the Army, I'd go to war for her in a second. And I'm not the only one who's that impressed with her. I've met many people through my work with

ADA, and anyone who's been touched by Susan feels the same way I do—she's the heart and soul of Delta's service-dog advocacy. Delta is so lucky to have her, and anyone who lives with a disability is lucky to have Susan on their side, too.

As I took Susan through DART's offices and she heard all the stories about Cody's lifesaving adventures with me and in the workplace, she suggested that I nominate him for Delta Society's Beyond Limits Award for Service Dog of the Year. Although I'd read something about the award, I hadn't really given it much thought. Of course I felt that Cody was deserving of some recognition, but I just didn't have the time to make a formal application. But Susan said that if I didn't nominate him, she would. Actually, she didn't have to do much convincing. I knew that there would be plenty of letters of support that would come from the people at DART, but I didn't know how *I* would make the time to do it.

So Susan asked Rob Knoebber, an associate of mine at Parsons, if he'd put the nomination package together, and he agreed to do so. Soon, the award nomination package was on its way to Delta. Included were letters from people who wrote about Dakota's alerting abilities and stories about his lifesaving deeds for me and others.

For instance, my colleague Dennis Echelberger wrote: "Dakota has brought another quality to the work arena. He is about the most gentle, rational soul on four paws."

"Dakota is Mike Lingenfelter's nonintrusive shadow," wrote Paul McGovern, another DART engineer. "One doesn't fully appreciate the dog's caliber until you see him without his service jacket. He's as frolicsome and troublesome as every average dog. It's only then that his obvious dedication to service becomes inspiring."

In his own letter, Rob wrote: " . . . to say that Dakota is just a well-disciplined and trained animal misses the essence that makes the Delta Society and the Service Dog program so viable. The dog's unselfish devotion to one person and his or her well-being is a kinship that can never be fathomed, just trust it . . . I have had the pleasure of seeing the best of the best—Dakota and Mike Lingenfelter."

And then there was a letter from Jessica Corn, the 11-year-old daughter of another of my colleagues, who wrote: "I think Dakota is a very special dog and should be given the award for the Best Service Animal—ever!"

A month later, in the summer of 1999, we were informed that Dakota was one of two national winners. I was thrilled that I was going to get to share all the wonderful things that Dakota was doing for me with the world.

▪   ▪   ▪

Winning the award didn't slow Cody down at all, and over the next several months, we managed to stay very busy at the office and in the community. One day, he yanked his leash out of my hand and ran into a cubicle to see one of his favorite people, an administrative aide named Betty. When he wouldn't leave her alone, she had an apprehensive look on her face—like everyone else in the office, she knew about Dakota's unique talents.

"Is he telling me something, Mike?" she asked.

"You know, Betty," I said, trying not to alarm her, "a few of us here in the office are of the opinion that if Dakota told us it was raining, we wouldn't look outside—we'd just go get an umbrella."

Betty understood what I was saying, and she went to her doctor that afternoon. Two days later, surgeons performed a procedure to clear arterial blockages in her heart.

Unbelievably, miraculously, Dakota was saving lives. I never expected his work to reach this heroic level—I just thought he'd get people to feel good about themselves.

One weekend we helped out at a workshop that was put on by DART and Service Dog Companions of Texas. This workshop was designed to teach service dogs, their human partners, and trainers how to deal safely and efficiently with light rail. It was a wonderful PR opportunity for DART. The dogs and their human partners were taught how to purchase tickets, where to wait for trains and how to board them, how to negotiate wheelchair ramps, and how to be safe in the stations. Many of these dogs were taking their first train ride, or dealing with crowds for the first time. Dakota was certainly the "old pro" in attendance, and I'm sure that we helped make it easier for the participants—the animals as well as their people. This fit right in with our AAT and ADA work.

Word of Dakota's work was getting around. The National Sertoma Club of Dallas chose Dakota as the Humanitarian of the Year, the first nonhuman recipient in history. Yet our lives didn't change all that much—we still went to the office every day to work on the DART light-rail project.

One day, Dave—one of our young, type-A engineers—popped into my cubicle to ask me a question. Dakota jumped up to greet him, and immediately hit him three times in the chest with his nose. Dave laughed and brushed him aside. I should have warned him to not ignore Dakota because that big red forepaw then proceeded to whack him pretty hard.

"Hey, what's wrong with you?" I asked him.

"Nothing," Dave said. "I'm fine."

"No, you're not."

Once again, I called Dr. Henderson, and he told me to bring Dave in. Luckily, Dave didn't need heart surgery, but it turned out that he did have a family heart history. He had a cholesterol reading of over 400, and went home with some anti-cholesterol drugs and blood-pressure medications.

Sadly, Dakota's messages weren't always interpreted correctly. An example of this happened when I was in Buffalo looking at some of the Parsons work under way. Dakota was less concerned about me than

75

about one of my officemates, a good-looking young man who was working on the project. I had to pull Cody out of his office several times. The last time I was in there, the man was down on the floor, petting Dakota and smiling.

"Are you okay?" I asked him, after retrieving Dakota one more time. And even though he seemed a little young to be concerned, I had to ask him anyway: "You don't have any heart problems, do you?"

Like everyone else in the office, he knew Dakota's story. "No, I'm fine," he said, enjoying his moments with Dakota. He looked like the typical all-American boy, and the two of them looked like they were in an ad from some fashion magazine.

"Do you have a dog?" I asked him.

"No, but I wish I did," he said. "Is this one available?"

I smiled. "I'll share him with you when I'm here. You may have to walk him once in a while, but they tell me that it's a great way to meet the women of the office building."

"Good—I could use a little help with that right now."

"How come I don't believe that?" I asked him, chuckling.

He laughed, too, a laugh that told me that there might be an element of truth to what he said.

Dakota still seemed reluctant to leave him, but it was time for us to head home. We flew back to Dallas that night. Over the weekend, I was told that the young man had committed suicide Saturday morning. The news upset me so much that I burst into tears. I guess you can't save them all, but Dakota was trying to tell me something there in Buffalo, and I missed it. I can't help but think that it was indeed something to do with this young man's heart. Maybe it wasn't physical, but his heart was definitely in some serious trouble.

■　　■　　■

On a happier note, Cody's award from Delta Society was getting a lot of attention from the media, and I was happy that he was getting the recognition he deserved. There were stories in dog magazines such as the *AKC Gazette* and *Dog World;* daily newspapers such as the *Dallas Morning News,* the *Seattle Times* and the *Chicago Tribune;* and other media such as *Men's Health* magazine, WGN radio, Lifetime, the Discovery Channel, Animal Planet, and on-line outlets. We were even in the *National Examiner.*

We almost gave one of the cable shows some exciting footage. Their video photographer was in Dr. Henderson's office with me when I had a severe angina attack. The photographer wanted to keep shooting, but Dr. Henderson ran him out of the examining room. I guess it would have made for good TV, but not from my point of view.

I was amazed to find out that there were so many dog and pet magazines out there. We were in most of them: *Dog News, Dog Fancy, ShowSight, The Golden Retriever Club of America Magazine* . . . the list goes on and on.

Men's Health magazine devoted its May 2000 issue to cardiac health, and ran a short piece on Dakota and his ability to alert on my angina attacks. A producer at *Good Morning America,* Patty Neger, saw the story and thought it would make a good segment for their show. Patty called me to make arrangements for a story—we'd be interviewed in Dallas and then take a trip to New York City to be on the show live. I thought that would be exciting, and we agreed that we'd try to do it in a couple of weeks.

■　　■　　■　　■　　■

CHAPTER NINE

If He's Sick, So Am I

It was always nice to have Dakota with me on the road. Of course, being my service dog, he went everywhere I went, which gave me great peace of mind and an occasional life-saving warning . . . and the added benefit of someone to talk to in my hotel room. But as far as roommates went, he did have his shortcomings—he didn't talk to me, he took up most of the bed, he snored, he was pretty disorganized, and he couldn't pack his own bag.

We were in Boston, a great city that I've always loved to visit. I'd been here for a week, working with the software supplier for the project I was overseeing for DART. But this had been a typical business trip—I'd spent all my time working, and all I got to see was the inside of a hotel room, the lobby, somebody's office, and the airport. I could have been in Paris for all I knew.

Cody and I were both anxious to get home—back to Nancy, Abbey, and familiar surroundings. I was also thinking about the upcoming week, when *Good Morning America* would be meeting us in Dallas. The plan was to have their cameras follow us around as we went about a normal day, and then fly us to New York for a studio interview. Since Cody's story had became known, we'd done a number of television pieces and a lot of magazine and newspaper interviews, but this was probably going to be the most significant. I was excited—I loved getting to share our story.

I was thinking about all of this as I started to pack. I gathered up Cody's toys, his treats, and his food and water bowls. His water bowl was empty, which was a little surprising, since I'd just filled it. *He must be really thirsty,* I thought.

"Want some more water, Code?" Now, I didn't actually expect him to answer, but I always asked him anyway. He looked up at me but didn't move. I guessed that he was really tuckered out from the long week. But that didn't tend to stop him—usually he was on his feet and under mine as I packed. Today he was neither.

I filled up his bowl with water and set it down in front of him. He drank it all quickly. I'd never seen him so thirsty and wondered what was going on. I decided to keep an eye on him that day. The nice thing about his being with me 24 hours a day was that I could watch him constantly without too much trouble.

As I've mentioned, Dakota was always a big hit wherever he went. He was an icebreaker and a nice diversion in a stressful workplace. Whether we were in Dallas or elsewhere, he'd do his therapy dog work at the same time that he was a service dog. I didn't mind sharing him—it made us both happy, and it gave others joy as well. It just reinforced my feeling that it was my duty to share him with as many people as I could.

At the software company in Boston, the women on the staff spent the week doting over him, keeping his water dish filled and walking him for me when I was tied up in meetings. Female attention, of course, was the incentive for my male co-workers to be so eager to help walk him at the office back in Dallas.

On this day, our last one in Boston, Dakota was really keeping everyone busy. He was drinking every bit of water they gave him. He just couldn't drink enough, and that meant that he had to make more

Dakota and his green frog by the pool.

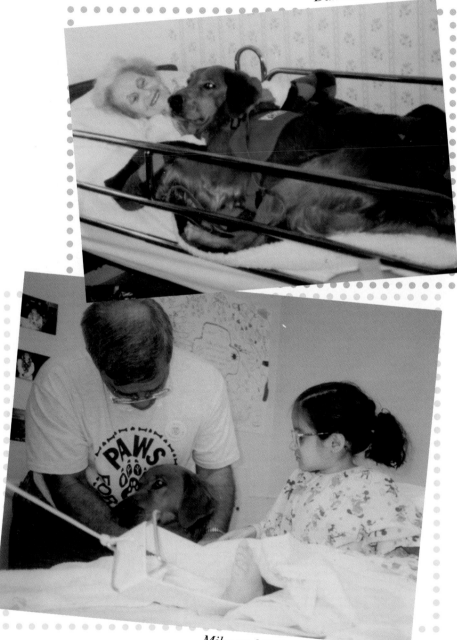

Dakota and Annette.

Mike and Dakota with Linda at the Shriners Children's Hospital, Houston.

Dakota and Mike at Shriners.

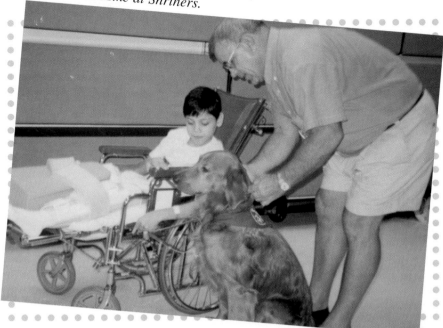

*Mike and Dakota visit with some
elementary school children.*

Dakota and kids at school on Pet Day.

*Dakota with the special children at
T. H. Rogers School, Houston.*

Nancy with Dakota, who's ready for his Christmas visit to the T. H. Rogers School.

Jan Hassler and Abbey at a training night for PAWS for Caring.

Dakota relaxes in his favorite spot in the Jeep.

*Mike, Dakota, and a buddy, swimming
in Lake Raystown, Pennsylvania.*

*Mike and Dakota with a
Foot of Ten Elementary School
teacher, Duncansville, Pennsylvania.*

*Granddaughter Megan and Dakota watch his
favorite movie,* Homeward Bound.

Abbey and Dakota waiting for the trick-or-treaters to arrive for Halloween.

*Mike (right) and Dakota, receiving the
Sertoma Club Award, Dallas.*

Dakota and Mike in the office, celebrating the
Delta Society National Service Dog Award.

Photo by Gay Glazbrook

Recovering at Auburn.

*Dakota (with his angel doll)
during treatment at Auburn.*

Granddaughter Becky nurtures Dakota after surgery.

Nancy gives Dakota a little TLC.

Teacher and student (Dakota and Olgivie).

Mike and Dakota, by the small animal clinic at Colorado State University.

Ogilvie and Dakota in the CSU waiting room.

Dakota's last picture before he returned to Heaven.

trips outside to relieve himself.

"Don't you give him any water at night?" one of the women teased me. "I've never seen him so thirsty. What did you feed him last night?"

"It must have been the garlic in his pasta," I told her, trying not to act too concerned, as we headed off to one more meeting.

Dakota wasn't moving too fast, and he plopped down under the table at my feet, in his normal position. It had been a long week here. Our purpose was to try to move the software people along—we were already three months behind schedule—and I wasn't sure that we'd made much progress on this trip. I suddenly found myself in the middle of what would normally be called a "healthy debate" about the scheduling.

Dakota jumped up to tell me that things were starting to turn "unhealthy." He started poking at and pulling on me. I didn't realize what was going on at first because I was too involved with the subject at hand . . . and too angry.

Mavash, one of the engineers in the meeting, knew Dakota and me well enough to take charge. "Come on, Mike, Dakota wants you out of here."

He was right. We stepped out of the meeting, or, should I say, Dakota *dragged* us out of the meeting. I took my medication and shortly after that had an angina attack. I found a quiet place to relax, and about an hour later I had the strength to rejoin the meeting.

"Mike, if we'd known that you were going to have a heart attack on us, we would have given you all the answers you wanted to hear right away," said Alan, the lead software developer.

"If I knew that's what it would take, I would have had it sooner," I said.

"Well, we want you to survive these meetings. We need your help to get this project done."

"Yeah, sure," I said, knowing that he was right, but playing along. "You'll get this done with or without me. I'm the oldest guy here, I come to work with a dog every day and disrupt the office, and I might just drop dead from a heart attack tomorrow. You don't need me."

Alan laughed. "That may be—but we do really like the dog."

That got us all laughing, and it was a good way to end the tough week.

There was a little buzz going on at the office after they witnessed Dakota's alert on me. I could feel it as we packed up and shook hands with everyone—they all seemed to have a little extra something as they patted Dakota on the head or stroked his neck.

But in spite of the excitement of all the good-byes to his new best friends at the office, Dakota still seemed a little quiet. I wished I knew what was going on with him, because this wasn't like him. He didn't seem sick, but he was tearing through the water and that wasn't normal.

Friday nights at the airport were always a little frantic, but no matter how much everyone was rushing to make their flights, it seemed that most of them took a look at Dakota and smiled. Occasionally, someone would stop to pet him and ask a question. After a tough business trip, I'm sure that a little Dakota on the way down the concourse was probably better for them than a visit to the airport cocktail lounge.

I flew home in my usual bulkhead seat with Dakota lying quietly at my feet. From there, he would receive visitors stopping by to pay their respects, like some sort of visiting royalty. He always had this peaceful countenance about him, combined with just enough tail-wagging golden retriever. It brought him pats on the head, ice cubes, and goodies from the food trays. After watching him in action for the past couple of years, I had to admit that it was a bit of a con job, but he certainly had it down.

When we landed in Dallas that evening, Dakota was still dragging a bit. We'd been traveling a lot lately, and I thought that he had probably picked up a bug along the way. I didn't want to take any chances, so I made an appointment to get him to the vet as soon as possible.

I don't like doctors' offices, and I feel the same way about veterinary clinics. Maybe the two are related in my mind on some psychological level, but I think that my dislike of vet clinics comes from the sounds and smells. I hate hearing dogs whining and crying and barking—they sound as if they've been abandoned. I'll tolerate it when I have to bring my dogs to get shots or some other routine treatment, but I didn't want to think about them sitting in a dog run, crying that sad bark, worrying about where I was.

But on Monday afternoon, I was hearing all those sounds and smelling all those smells as we sat in Dr. Krug's reception area. Dr. Harold Krug was relatively new in our lives. Four months earlier, we ended up in his office when our previous veterinarians weren't having any luck solving Dakota's chronic ear infection. When Dr. Krug succeeded, he became our regular vet. He had a ready smile, a great manner with our golden retrievers, and a total understanding of how important any service dog is in the life of their human partner.

He also became a pretty good friend, and we'd needle one another mercilessly.

"Did they teach you that at Texas A&M, or did you read it in some book?" I'd ask him. "Oh, I forgot, you Aggies don't read much, do you?"

"We *have* to read," he'd answer. "You Penn State guys have already taken all the books with pictures."

"Where's Julie, anyway? She's the only reason we come here," I'd fire back. I knew that Julie, Dr. Krug's wife, was the one who ran things around the clinic. She always found a way to squeeze me in for an appointment, even when there were none available.

Dakota had a way of bringing special people into our lives, and Julie and Harold were two more. Dakota had become a very special friend to them, too, enough so that Dr. Krug had nominated Dakota for the Texas Veterinary Medical Association's Animal Hall of Fame. Nancy and I hadn't been in to see them for a couple of weeks—which seemed like a long time between veterinary visits for us. Julie greeted us all in the reception area, and Dakota was happy to see her.

Dr. Krug joined us. He just barely said hello to us, turning his attention to Dakota immediately. "Hey, Cody, how're you doing, buddy?" Dr. Krug patted him on the head, and Cody's tail wagged very slowly. We all saw that Dakota was a little lethargic, which really seemed to knock the doctor down. That scared me.

Dr. Krug took Dakota's leash and led us all back into an examination room. "Well, he seems a little 'blah,'" he said, as he went through a physical exam. "But his temperature is normal, all his surface lymph nodes are normal, and I'm not finding anything unusual. I'd like to do a couple of things in the back, take some blood, do an x-ray."

"Do whatever you need to do," I told him. "Dakota's just not himself, and I'd like to see what we can find. Do you want me to come with you?"

"No, that's okay. My assistant Brad is back there. He can help me." Dr. Krug started to lead Dakota out of the room, but, as always, Dakota didn't want to leave me behind. I gave him the release command, but he was still reluctant.

"It's okay, Dakota, kennel up," I repeated. As Dr. Krug led him away, Cody kept looking back over his shoulder at me.

Why does Dr. Krug seem so restrained? I wondered. *What's going on here?* It was almost 6 o'clock. All the other clients were gone, so Nancy and I waited out in the reception area. Julie was going back and forth between the front counter and the back room. I didn't like the fact that she was trying to make small talk with us, like she was putting on some kind of a brave front. We weren't sure what to expect, but Dakota was just acting a little quiet and drinking a lot of water. How bad could it be?

Please, just let it be something he ate, I kept praying. We weren't expecting anything major—after all, Cody and I had already challenged death a few times—but I think it's fair to say that we were a little concerned. After a while, the door to the exam room finally opened, and Dr. Krug waved us in. Dakota was sitting there, peacefully.

Dr. Krug had tears in his eyes. "I didn't want to be right. I wanted to find something else, but it's cancer."

Thoughts fired rapidly through my brain: *Cancer?! Cancer now, after all he's been through? After all we've been through? How can this be? Where are you, God? How can you let this happen to him? All Dakota has ever done is help people. How can you do this to me, God? To us? To my family?*

I was suddenly angry. I wanted to hit something. If Dakota has cancer, *I* have cancer.

"It's a death sentence, Mike," Dr. Krug said, somewhere through my anger. "I'm not going to lie to you. You're looking at four to six weeks, maybe three months, tops. I didn't want to find a tumor, but here it is." He put the x-ray up on the light screen: The tumor was a large white circle in the middle of the picture. It looked like a headlight coming straight at me, full-speed ahead.

I could barely speak. "Is he in pain?"

"I don't think he's in great pain right now, but I'm sure that he's uncomfortable," Dr. Krug said. He went on to explain that the tumor, which was the size of a softball, was pushing up against Cody's heart from its position between the heart and the lungs.

"Mike, when you told us over the phone that he was drinking an abnormal amount of water, this was my first frightening thought," Dr. Krug said. "Any vet in this day and age will tell you that a golden retriever drinking that much water is trouble. It's because the dog is 'calcified.' Golden retrievers are predisposed to lymphoma, and when cancer takes over the lymph system, it causes *hypercalcemia,* or too much calcium in the blood, which can cause problems in the liver and kidneys. The body tries to help flush it out with a high water intake.

"We won't have the bloodwork back until tomorrow, but I'll bet anything that he's got a calcium reading off the chart." He showed Nancy and me a couple of additional x-rays. The tumor was very evident in all of them—it was in the lymph node in front of the heart, and surgery couldn't be performed there.

I was in a daze. *My world may as well stop if Dakota can't be a part of it,* I thought.

However, Dr. Krug had already taken charge. "After looking at the first x-ray, I went ahead and did some things. Because the tumor is so large, and the x-rays show me exactly where it is, I stuck a needle in there and took an aspirate. The cytology report will show if it's lymphoma or not—but I'm already pretty sure that's what we're looking at here.

"We can help him be comfortable," he continued, "and I admit that I'm trying to buy some time for him, and also for you, so you can come to accept this. If we're aggressive, we might have a chance to extend his life. I don't want to lose a day waiting for lab work to come back telling us the obvious. So I went ahead and gave him a dose of chemotherapy, a drug called Vincristine. If it's not cancer, then all that's happened is that we've wasted a dose of chemotherapy. I also gave him a heavy dose of steroids, drugs that have been 'screaming effective' in the past in these types of cancers. And I gave some antibiotics, too, because the chemotherapy can really compromise the immune system."

"How can it be any worse?" I finally asked.

He shrugged his shoulders. "The lab results might surprise us—but I doubt it. I'm pretty sure we're looking at lymphoma. And that's about as nasty as it gets."

"Is there any hope? Can anyone help him?" I asked.

"We haven't had much luck with this type of cancer here at our clinic, either in treatment or via surgery. But I know a veterinarian here in Dallas who specializes in cancer in dogs. Let me call her tomorrow and see what she thinks. But I don't think we should be optimistic."

Nancy and I tried to comfort one another and hug Dakota at the same time. But she and I were both feeling angry and helpless. We drove home in a daze. Dakota just laid on the backseat and didn't move. On the way home, I thought about what I could do to let Dakota know how much I loved him. I couldn't even think about going back to work—I just wanted to spend the time left with Dakota. I needed to hold him and feel his warmth against me for as long as possible.

I can't remember too much about what happened when we got home. I just wanted to die. This news was making me search for the words to describe my love for Dakota, but I couldn't find them. My love for him, and his for me, was spiritual. Without him, my life would have no meaning or purpose, either spiritually or physically.

That night, I e-mailed the news to several close friends:

> *Please be advised that Dakota will be retiring.... We have just learned that he has terminal cancer. Treatment with cancer drugs, to help him have a better quality of life in the near term, has been started.*
>
> *I know that each of you will keep him in your prayers and that Dakota understands that he is loved by all of you. Nancy and I thank each of you for your understanding of the fact that I can no longer let him work. He must be given the time left to be just a happy golden retriever.*

■　　■　　■

The next morning, I called Patty Neger at *Good Morning America*. I gave her the news about Dakota and told her that we wouldn't be coming to New York. However, she told me that their field producer was already en route to Dallas, so I agreed to think about doing some very limited taping here with Dakota.

"Mike, I want to help you and Dakota," Patty said to me on the telephone. "If there's anything that can be done, any treatment to be found, any drug that can help, we can go on national TV to find it."

We'd never even met Patty or anyone else at ABC in person, but she was touched by Dakota's ordeal and was crying as she hung up. Less than two hours later, she called back. "I've talked to Marty Becker, our staff veterinarian for *GMA,* and he can help," she told me. "He called his friend Dr. Greg Ogilvie at the Colorado State

University Animal Cancer Clinic, and set up an appointment for you Monday morning."

"That's great," I said. "What do I have to do?"

"You don't have to do anything," Patty said. "Just get on the airplane. *GMA* is picking up the tab. All we ask is that you let our producer fly with you and shoot the story."

That seemed like a fair trade, so I agreed.

Patty continued, "And if the doctor will let Dakota do it, we'll fly you from Colorado to New York for the show, and then home to Dallas."

I told her that that was up to the doctors. I just wanted to do what was best for Dakota. We agreed on all the particulars, as much as we could at this point in time, and Patty told me that she'd call me back with the travel arrangements.

Early that afternoon, the phone rang again. It was Harold Krug, and he wanted to see us right away. "What did you find out?" I asked him.

"Let's talk about it when you get here," he said.

Oh no, I thought. *How could this be anything but bad news?*

Nancy and I made it to the clinic in a few minutes, expecting bad news, but hoping for some positive word.

"Mike, it's what we thought," Dr. Krug told us. "Cancer, T-cell lymphoma, the worst. The blood work shows that Cody's calcium is elevated by nearly 50 percent, so that certainly supports the lymphoma finding."

I looked around the room, and Julie and Nancy were both crying. "What's next?" I asked, fighting back my own tears.

"Well, probably the most we can hope for is just to keep him comfortable. We'll keep him on the chemo once a week—that's a start. And if we keep giving him steroids and antibiotics, that won't hurt either."

"What about your cancer vet here in town?"

"She told me that she's been through this too many times," Dr. Krug said. "She's lost so many dogs with this type of cancer that she just won't take on another one. She's burned out. But she did tell me about the protocol to begin on Dakota."

I told him about our appointment at CSU that coming Monday. "That's great," he said. "Dr. Ogilvie is one of the veterinary world's 'deep breathers,' an icon in the field. You're seeing the world's best animal cancer doctor in the world's best animal cancer facility."

Julie looked at her husband: "You're going with them, you know."

He smiled weakly and nodded. "I know."

Dr. Krug was a part of the family at this point, and as far as I was concerned, it was crucial that he come along and get the background and treatment suggestions. I was glad that he and Julie felt the same way.

Julie stepped out of the room for a few minutes while Dr. Krug administered the steroids and antibiotics. She came back with a smile through the tears. "God is telling us that you're supposed to go with Dakota and Mike," she told her husband. "What are the odds that you wouldn't have any appointments this Monday? Well, you don't. And what are the odds that I could get you on a plane at the last minute, with a mileage award ticket? Well, I did. This was just meant to be."

Through all of these events, the Krugs kept talking about how special Dakota was, how he just grew on everyone. But something else was going on here, too. It was pretty obvious to Nancy and me that Dr. Krug was just as worried about me as he was about Dakota.

"Listen, Mike," he continued, "I don't want to sugarcoat this—it's pretty grim. But let's take some good news from all of this. For one thing, because you're so in tune with Dakota and know instantly when something is wrong with him, we've gotten a jump on this. We got that chemo and the steroids into him the moment we saw a tumor. Also, the cancer involvement seems to be limited to just that one lymph node. That doesn't mean that the others aren't involved, but we didn't see any on the x-rays, and we didn't feel any on the physical exam. Most of these cancers are multicentric, but right now this one doesn't seem to be. That might make it a little more treatable."

Finally, we had something to grab on to. I was scared, but this was a small ray of hope. And although I was grabbing on, I had to be realistic—after all, we were still dealing with cancer.

■　　■　　▧　　■　　■

CHAPTER TEN

The Man and the Mountain

There was little doubt that Dr. Greg Ogilvie was "The Man" and the Animal Cancer Center (ACC) at Colorado State University (CSU) in Fort Collins was "The Mountain."

If your dog or cat has cancer, this is the place to be. The ACC is widely acknowledged as the world's leading research and treatment facility for cancer in animals, and Dr. Ogilvie is the world's leading authority. The work being done on animals at CSU also had profound implications in the field of human cancer.

Nancy and I found out that Dr. Ogilvie was a great believer in the human-animal bond, which pretty much sold us on him before we even showed up there. We'd heard over and over again about his passion for his work, and his compassion for his patients and their people.

Everyone we spoke to about him said he was a legend, larger than life.

He was even better in person.

We had a bit of an entourage as we walked through the door of the clinic that morning with Dakota—there was the three-person crew from *Good Morning America* lugging a TV camera and a boom mike on their shoulders, Dana Durrance from the Argus Institute's Support Program,

Dr. Harold Krug, and me.

Dr. Ogilvie approached the group and introduced himself by saying, "Somebody here has to be Dakota's dad."

"That's me, sir," I said. We humans all exchanged a few pleasantries, and then Dr. Ogilvie got down on his hands and knees on the waiting-room floor and greeted Dakota as if he were a long lost friend.

"Hey, Dakota, how are you doing?" His hands were stroking Dakota's head, neck, back, and chest. I bet that Cody was already feeling better. The doctor did a quick initial exam on the floor, checking Dakota's vital signs and the like, and then led us back into an exam room.

I already knew that I was seeing the best in action.

"How are *you* holding up, Mike?" he asked me.

"It's pretty rough, Dr. Ogilvie," I told him. "I can't lie to you—this big guy means the world to me, in many different ways."

"First of all, call me Greg. You're now part of the family here."

Yes, he is the very best, I thought.

"Cancer is an emotional disease, Mike. It steals hope, and once you lose hope, your life is violated and you feel totally out of control."

He was right about that.

"By the time people get to us with their pets, they're scared to death. They're afraid that there are no options left for them and their pet, that it's time for the holy water."

I could understand that. "Things do seem a little grim—three months to live kind of got our attention."

"Well, let's not kid about this," he said. "Cancer is the number-one natural cause of death in dogs and cats in the U.S. As for the type of cancer that Dakota has, the average dog will live only a few months unless they get some prompt care."

I was sitting down with Dakota's head in my lap, trying unsuccessfully to hold back the tears. I've never been good at that when it comes to Dakota.

Dr. Ogilvie saw my emotion and tried to reassure me. "Remember,

I see more lymphoma in a couple of weeks' time than most practitioners do in a lifetime. That gives us a real advantage. Believe it or not, cancer is the most curable of all common diseases."

I'd never heard anyone say that about cancer, and here I was hearing it from the world's leading authority. I was riveted to Dr. Ogilvie's words.

"There isn't a single patient that we can't help," Dr. Ogilvie continued, "and we're going to help Dakota. We're going to get him back to you with a minimum of downtime, ready to be back in your life soon. We've come a long way. Back in the day that I was educated, there were very few options for cancer patients. The mentality was that cancer is a disease, that you either cure it or you die from it. The reality today is that it doesn't have to be that way anymore. If we can't cure it, many cancers can be controlled for a long period of time.

"And why is that so hard to grasp? We're now defining *cancer* as a chronic disease. You think nothing of having a heart valve replaced if you have heart disease, or getting a kidney transplant or dialysis if you have renal disease—the comparisons can go on and on. We can put cancer in remission. It may take time, and it may require a number of different treatment modalities that can be difficult, but the truth is that we can do something here, much more than just make the patient comfortable in preparation for death. We don't accept that. That's not what we do. So there you have it, Mike. That's my pep talk, and now it's time to get to work."

My heart was pounding away—but it must have been pounding in a good way, because Dakota wasn't alerting on me. I wanted to jump up out of my chair and shout, "I believe!"

■   ■   ■

The first step in examining Cody was to get a chest x-ray to compare to the pictures taken the previous week by Dr. Krug. While we were waiting for the film to develop, Dr. Ogilvie told us a little more about how they did things at the ACC. The therapy program took place on two levels: The first was in meeting the medical needs of the patients for palliative care (pain and nausea control), nutritional support, or actual cancer therapy; the second was directed at meeting the nonmedical needs of both the patient and the caregiver (usually the human partner). As Dr. Ogilvie said, "A lot of people don't realize that animals need just as much emotional support and compassionate care as human cancer patients, and so do their caregivers."

For the caregiver, the support system at CSU reflected the concern for the animals and the people, including their physical and spiritual needs. The Argus Institute, affiliated with the ACC and the school, provides support and counseling services for families. It also teaches veterinary students about communication, crisis intervention, and grief counseling. We'd be leaning heavily upon them as we helped Dakota fight his battles.

Dr. Ogilvie went out to get the x-ray film for us to look at together. "Hey, look at this," he said, putting the current picture up on the light screen next to the one from the previous week. "Wow, this is really good." He pointed at the old x-ray: "That bad gnarly guy right there, it's almost gone . . . there's just a little bit left, but not much at all. I think that we can thank Dr. Krug for giving us a nice head start last week. Getting that first dose of chemo into Dakota so quickly was crucial."

Dr. Krug smiled. It had to be nice to be validated, to hear that he'd done the right thing, and that it worked. And to hear it from Dr. Ogilvie had to make him feel especially good. I smiled right back at Harold.

Dr. Ogilvie was already making good on his promises. Although we hadn't had too much hope when we arrived, now there seemed to be some. "When you come back on Monday, we'll do some blood work and some other tests that will hopefully back up what we see here. If there are no surprises there, we'll want to give Dakota more than just traditional chemotherapy. That, in and of itself, won't be enough to save him."

Since Dr. Krug had given Cody a chemotherapy dose last week, there was nothing for Dr. Ogilvie to do for a few days. He saw no reason why Dakota couldn't travel to New York for *Good Morning America,* but he wanted him back for a month of treatments beginning the following Monday.

"You know, Mike, cancer teaches me on a daily basis that life is a chain of moments that need to be celebrated," Greg said. "Cancer is a big exclamation point that reminds us of the vibrancy and importance of life. That's why you should go on *Good Morning America* and tell Dakota's story to the world. That message needs to get out there. People need to hear about the human-animal bond at its finest, and that's what you two represent. We want people to hear about how important companion animals are to their humans, and we want people to hear about how important it is to improve the quality of life for animals and people alike. There's a reason why this is happening to you and Dakota—maybe it's so you can help get that message out there."

He gave me a hug. "We had a good start today. Travel safe, and we'll see you Monday."

We said our good-byes and headed to the airport. Dr. Krug was flying back to Dallas, but I knew that he had to be feeling good about his role in all of this. It was his swift response with the Vinchristine chemotherapy a week earlier that had helped get the treatment process under way.

"Harold, I can't tell you how much it means to have you come along with us," I told him as we sped down I-25 toward the Denver airport. "Your support and your efforts are really making a difference. We're lucky to have you on our team. We've felt that way all along, and Greg saw that today. He was happy with what you've done."

"It was nice to hear him say that, sure," Harold said, "but that means nothing to me unless Dakota gets better. Julie and I will do whatever it takes and help you with whatever you need, you know that."

Yes, I did know that. The Krugs are truly exceptional people.

■   ■   ■

Cody and I flew to New York. Even though it had been a long day, Dakota seemed to be getting his energy back. ABC sent a car to pick us up at the airport and take us to our hotel in Times Square, right across the street from the *GMA* studios.

After the long trip, Dakota needed a "comfort break." I'd been to New York enough to know that it wasn't always easy to find a place to walk a dog in the middle of Manhattan, so I headed to the hotel's bell stand to look for some guidance.

"Where can I find some grass around here?" I asked.

The porter paused for a second, as he seemed to size me up. Then he replied: "Hey man, you're in the middle of Times Square. You can buy it from just about anyone out there."

That was pretty funny. *Dakota, I've a feeling we're not in Plano anymore,* I thought. Even during that difficult time, we found that there were things to laugh about.

We went to dinner at Carmine's, which was a crowded Italian restaurant just off Times Square. Dakota, sitting quietly at my feet as we ate at the bar, drew a lot of attention, and I'm sure that we built up the audience for *GMA* the next morning after all the questions we answered.

The next morning, Cody and I walked across the street to the show. Dakota, as usual, created quite a stir in the green room (the waiting room for the guests). Patty Neger was there to meet us, and she started to cry as she greeted Dakota for the first time. She had a big hug for me, too, and as so often happened because of Dakota, I felt like Patty and I were already close friends.

"How was the trip in? Is the hotel okay?" she asked. I told her the story about looking for grass, and even though she was a New Yorker working in Times Square, she got a kick out of that.

The hosts, Charles Gibson and Diane Sawyer, dropped by separately to say hello and ask for Cody's latest medical report. Charles was going to be doing the interview, but Diane was asking just as many questions, since she did the narrative for the taped piece from Plano and CSU. Charles and Diane were both taken with Dakota, his presence, and his story. Every staffer wanted to pet Cody, and he greeted them all in his trademark tail-wagging fashion.

Another of the guests on *GMA* that morning was William Shatner of *Star Trek* fame. He was also very curious about Dakota, and listened intently as I told him the story. He asked questions along the way and shook his head in amazement at the details. When I was done, he was obviously touched by our story and very taken with Dakota. He told me, "Listen, if this is ever made into a movie, promise me that you'll call me about playing your role. This is a great story." And then Captain James T. Kirk of the Starship Enterprise, the Universe's greatest intergalactic warrior, cried, too.

A few minutes later, we were on the air. Charles Gibson introduced our story: "'A faithful friend is the medicine of life.' That is a quotation from the Bible that very aptly describes the special relationship between our next two guests."

The story that was taped at home in Plano and at the Animal Cancer Clinic in Fort Collins played first. When it was done, Charles conducted the live interview. He seemed even more fascinated by the story the second time around. He held us over into the next half-hour, which didn't usually happen in the world of network morning shows. Dakota slept at my feet through most of it, looking up once for some attention. His green frog was right there under his nose, where it always was.

I'd looked up into the TelePrompTer at one point and had seen Diane's name in the script, too. I wondered why she wasn't on with us. But as we were leaving, Diane came up to tell me that she was so moved by Dakota's story that she wouldn't have been able to hold her composure. Then she gave us both a big hug, which was probably the best thing for all of us anyway.

I thought the show went well, and Patty loved it. Then it was time to say our good-byes to everyone, and it was hugs and tears all around as we headed for home.

Once at Kennedy Airport, Cody and I went to the American Airlines counter to check in. The ticket agent saw us and broke into a big smile. "I saw you this morning on TV, and I'm still crying," she said, coming out from behind the counter to give Dakota a big hug. "I'm going to be remembering you in my prayers. You can beat this cancer thing, and I'll send you all my strength, too." It seemed as if she'd been waiting for us. She took my ticket and handed me a boarding pass for a first-class seat. That was nice—because of Dakota, we occasionally got bumped up. "Now you head right for the gate," she said. "They're waiting for you."

Waiting for me? I'm an hour-and-a-half early, I thought.

We went to the gate, and when we got there, the gate agent seemed to be waiting for us, too. "Come with me, Mr. Lingenfelter." No one else was boarding yet, but we followed her down the jetway to the airplane. She ushered me to my seat, and there were pillows and blankets on the floor for a bed for Cody, along with a crystal bowl filled with ice cubes. The agent gave Dakota a pat on the head, and gave me a wink. "Enjoy your flight home," she said. "We want you both to have all your strength for the coming weeks." I thought that this had to be Patty Neger's doing—it seemed that we had another special member of the family now.

Back home, I finally had some time to gather my thoughts. Looking ahead, the plan was for Nancy, Abbey, Dakota, and me to start driving Sunday the nearly 1,000 miles back to Fort Collins. We were going to be gone for four weeks to get Dakota through this cancer treatment, so I had to get home and make some arrangements for my work.

As I looked back at everything that had gone on in the last ten days, we had much to be thankful for, despite everything we'd already been through. We'd met a few new heroes, some new members of Dakota's team. It was evident that we were truly blessed.

■   ■   ■   ■   ■

CHAPTER ELEVEN

The Bond

No one I'd ever met in my entire life had made a greater first impression on me than Dr. Greg Ogilvie had. His words had continually rung in my ears for days: *"Cancer is a big exclamation point that reminds us of the vibrancy and importance of life."* Greg challenged me to get out and tell Dakota's story to the world so that we could really illustrate what the human-animal bond was all about. That was something that would inspire me for the rest of my days.

I'd been living the reality of the human-animal bond since that very first walk I took with Dakota. He gave me back my freedom, which was something that I'd taken for granted before my disabling illness. And, seemingly overnight, he made my life better, just by being there for me when I needed help physically, mentally, or spiritually. From those first walks around our neighborhood, I could see that dogs in general and Cody in particular could bring something special to people's lives. When Dakota and I got involved with Paws for Caring back in Houston, our work with animal-assisted therapy drove home how much relationships with animals mean to people. I'd been a firm believer ever since.

Greg had told me that there was a reason this was happening to Dakota—which gave Nancy and me even more resolve to help Dakota get well. We now had a mission, a purpose. It took Greg to officially verbalize it, but it also resonated through all of the people Cody had touched—from little Linda in the Shriners Hospital for Children, to the kids at T. H. Rogers School, to Annette, the wonderful woman in the nursing home who died with her arm around Dakota.

At home the next morning, I got on my computer and found the Animal Cancer Center's (ACC) Website. After a little surfing, I found a link to the FAQs (Frequently Asked Questions), which were written by Greg himself. A lot of it sounded like the very things we'd discussed during our visit, but a couple of statements really jumped out at me:

> When we face the diagnosis of cancer in a beloved pet, it is even more difficult, for we must make important and life-changing deci-sions for creatures that rely totally on our own judgments for their well-being. . . . We have experienced their love as unconditional, and we seek through our own decision-making process to provide for them the quality and dignity of life that we know they deserve.

This was exactly what I'd been wrestling with ever since I'd seen that first x-ray in Dr. Krug's office, and it would continue to be my pri-mary thought as we moved through the cancer treatment process at CSU. I wanted to do what was right by Dakota. I couldn't and wouldn't let him suffer. I read on and found comfort and solace as the words seemed to jump off my computer screen at me:

> *Compassionate care* is the single most important operative term in cancer medicine. It is the outward manifestation of caring with the science through the heart and is a response by the veterinary health-care team based on an understanding and appreciation of the bond . . . seek out compassionate care provided by people that recognize and value the magic you and your pet share. It is then that you and your pet will daily live in the hope and the wonder of that precious relationship we all know, yet find beyond our abilities to explain . . . the bond. (© Gregory K. Ogilvie, 2000)

The bond. This was really what it was all about. It was that special, sometimes magical, relationship that exists between people and their pets, often coming about because of their involvement in our daily lives. Greg got it; he saw it every day. But Dakota and I *lived* the human-animal bond: We experienced it in our daily lives through our support of one another, we saw it in our work in animal-assisted therapy, and we worked for it as advocates for service dogs and their accessibility rights. That bond was going to help carry us as Nancy and I strove to make the right decisions for Dakota. The first decision that we made was right and continued to be right: We'd brought him to the best facility, and we were working with the best people—there was absolutely no doubt about that.

ACC is part of the Colorado State University Veterinary Teaching Hospital. Its stated mission is "to improve prevention and treatment of cancer in animals and humans." Each year, the center manages more than 7,000 appointments (1,500 new patients) and thousands of consultation calls from veterinarians around the world, making it the largest such clinic in the world. The growth of this center, from a small service unit into one of the world's best-known treatment and research facilities, was closely linked to the increase of the occurrence of cancer in dogs. According to ACC, dogs develop cancer at about the same rate as humans, and cancer accounts for nearly half of all deaths in dogs over the age of ten. Interestingly, ACC says that golden retrievers are among the breeds with the highest incidence of cancer. But we weren't going to let Dakota be just another statistic.

■　　■　　■

"Here's what we know," Greg said, as we began that first day in the exam room. "We've all seen the pictures by now, we all know that Dakota has a tumor of the lymph node, or *lymphoma.* Historically, Dakota's got a few things going against him as we begin—when it comes to cancer, male dogs do worse than females, and large breeds do worse than small breeds. And we already know that golden retrievers have a greater incidence of cancer than average. With treatment, the average dog will live four to five months."

Nancy and I chimed in simultaneously: "He's not an average dog." So we knew *that* was in Cody's favor. Another thing he had going for him was that the tumor had been shrinking ever since that first dose of chemotherapy was administered by Dr. Krug.

The first level of cancer therapy was to meet the medical needs of the patient. To get that under way, Greg ordered up a battery of tests, a routine history, and a physical examination. After two days of tests, the results had few surprises and a bit of good news. The official terminology for Cody's illness was "an anterior mediastinal lymphoma without evidence of organ involvement."

"I think the fact that there is no evidence of organ involvement is a small victory, and we can celebrate that," Greg said. "Our plan now should be to try to control the tumor in his chest, and then to attack any microscopic amounts of cancer that may be present elsewhere in his body."

He then outlined a 25-week program of chemotherapy and radiation, and a continuing holistic regimen to include nutritional supplements, herbal treatments, and acupuncture. The first four weeks, which included 15 radiation treatments and chemotherapy, would be at CSU. After that, Dr. Krug could continue and complete the chemotherapy at his clinic in Plano.

"I think that this is our best treatment program at this time. This approach gives us a good chance for sustained control of the disease," Greg told me. "It's new enough that it's still a bit unproven, but we're having success with this regimen on a lot of other patients with the same type of cancer."

The good news of the day contrasted with a problem I was having with my job. My superiors were being very insistent that I needed to be in the office in Dallas next week. We were having a critical meeting for the project, and if I wanted to come back to Colorado for the last three weeks of Dakota's treatments, I first needed to train my deputy manager to take over my duties at work.

This raised two big questions: First, what was I going to do without Dakota? And second, what was Dakota going to do without me? Nancy and I had talked about it on the entire trip to CSU. My first reaction was that I'd just walk away from my job—if they were going to force me to choose between them and Dakota, I'd retire on the spot. But then I told Greg about my situation.

"Mike, you know that Dakota's going to be in the best hands here," he said. "I can't speak for your job, and I can't speak for your needs for him in his service-dog role. But I can guarantee you that he'll have only the best of care and attention here for that week. In fact, if it's okay with you, I'll even take him home with me at night. He'll become a part of our family for that week." Greg was already working on the second phase of treatment: meeting the nonmedical needs of the patient and the caregiver.

"Greg, that's a wonderful offer," I replied, "and I can't think of anyone else I'd rather entrust him to. Let me think about it overnight. I mean, maybe this is all a sign that it's time for me to retire."

After thinking for a moment, Greg said, "You know, maybe this would be a good time to introduce you to the people at Changes. Maybe a little counseling will provide you with some comfort and will help clear your head so that you can make some decisions about what's going on with *you.*"

Changes: Support for People and Pets was one of the nation's first pet-loss support programs, offering counseling for individuals and families as they struggled with the reality of cancer in a beloved pet. It was part of the Argus Institute for Families and Veterinary Medicine at CSU, a partner of the ACC, and was staffed by veterinarians and mental health-care professionals. The institute also provided training for veterinarians and staff and mental-health professionals to deal in an enlightened and sensitive manner with those issues of grief and loss so often associated with chronic illness. This infusion of holistic healing, melded with the very best of human compassion, veterinary medicine, and mental-health care, is what's known as "Bond-Centered Practice."

I'd met Dana Durrance from Changes the week before. She was a clinical psychologist who worked with CSU's clinicians and staff to facilitate the sensitive handling of the hospital's medical cases. Throughout the course of her day, she'd circulate in and out of the clinic, visiting with the people and families who were there with their pets. We ran into her as soon as we went back out to the waiting room, and she could read that we were a little troubled. We filled her in on what was going on, both here with Dakota and back home in Texas.

"What can we do to help you?" Dana asked. "You're not alone in this fight, you know. We can be good listeners or a shoulder to cry on, whatever you need." She also went on to ask if we had everything we needed away from the hospital. Nancy and I assured her that we did.

"I'm amazed at how in tune this town is with what goes on here at the Cancer Clinic," I told her. "The people at the hotel and in the restaurants and the grocery stores . . . they're all so friendly and supportive." In just a short time here, we'd seen that the community formed a sort of psycho-social safety net for family members of pets being treated at ACC. We chatted about all the things that the Changes program did. Empowered by people like Dana and embraced by people like Greg, Changes certainly fulfilled that second level of cancer care that Greg told us about. Over the next few weeks, we saw Dana constantly. It seemed that every time we needed her, she was there, and that every time we needed to be alone, she could feel that as well. Nancy and I knew that we could count on her at any time.

It came as no surprise that we put in a lot of time in the ACC's waiting room. From time to time, one of the counselors from Changes would come through and visit, but most of the time we were chatting with each other or reading newspapers or magazines or talking to others like us, anxiously awaiting the next report on their beloved pet. It was only our second day here, and we were still looking around a lot, getting to know some of the staff and a few of our fellow patients. We visited with others in the waiting room, sharing the connection that bonded us like warriors who were fighting very similar battles. No one wanted to be here, but we all seemed to find comfort with one another right away, knowing that sometime soon we might need others to share in our happy victories or devastating defeats.

We found solace in each other's stories. Nancy and I found ourselves sharing our histories with total strangers who had become part of Dakota's great extended family. Questions flew back and forth: "How's it going? How's your dog doing? What program is he on? Where are you from? How long have you been here? How much longer are you staying? What are you finding out here? Which doctors are you seeing?"

A prime topic was always the innovative aspect of the treatment programs at ACC, specifically its inclusion of complementary therapies such as acupuncture. Dr. Robinson was the veterinary acupuncturist at CSU—but she was also a practicing osteopathic physician and medical acupuncturist for humans as well. She was the only acupuncturist teaching at a veterinary college in North America, and her course was so popular that there was a one-year wait to get into her class.

Cody lay there peacefully for the treatment, which appeared to be pretty much the same as in humans. Small needles were placed at various points along his meridians (pathways in the body along which the body's energy is believed to flow) to stimulate nerves and the immune system. "The objectives are pain relief, immune stimulation, and overall improvement in energy and vitality," Dr. Robinson told us. "I think that acupuncture is a great alternative treatment for veterinarians who get tired of having drugs and surgery as their only options, especially in chronic pain cases."

"I haven't really seen Cody demonstrate any pain," I said. "I wish he could tell us if he's hurting, and where he's hurting."

"Have you ever worked with an animal communicator?" Dr. Robinson asked.

"No. I'm not really sure what they do."

"Well, in simplest terms, they facilitate communication between you and your pet," she said. "If you're interested in finding out more about that kind of thing, I'll give you a phone number when we're done here."

■　　■　　■

She wasn't Dr. Dolittle, and "Talk to the Animals" wasn't a class at the school of veterinary medicine—in fact, the powers-that-be at CSU stopped short of calling it heresy, asking Dr. Brenda McClelland to keep her talents as an animal communicator separate from her job as a staff veterinary specialist in ophthalmology. To complicate matters further, she was also a certified practitioner of Reiki and Healing Touch, holistic work that was also totally separate—again, at the school's request—from her duties at CSU. Reiki and Healing Touch are considered forms of alternative medicine, with practitioners using their hands to manipulate the flow of energy in the body on physical, mental, emotional, and spiritual levels.

We had to call her at home and set up an appointment outside of CSU. I was curious about it all, but I didn't really know what to expect. Brenda put me at ease right away, telling me that 50 percent of her sessions were spent dealing with sick or injured animals, 40 percent with behavioral issues, and the remaining 10 percent were just for visits. I intentionally didn't tell her anything about Dakota, other than that we were here for treatment at the hospital. As it turned out, Brenda was already meeting with another CSU patient and their family that night at the same hotel, and she came to see us in our room immediately afterwards.

After some brief introductions, I said, "I don't know much about animal communicators."

"Well, I don't like the term *communicator* per se," she answered, "because I do the exact same thing in my human sessions as I do in my animal sessions, and I get the same information off the human that I get off the animal. After all, they don't call me a 'human communicator.' *I'd* like to call it 'higher-self communication,' which deals with the subconscious mind, in contact with all other subconscious minds in the world. It's similar to how a mother knows when their child is in danger, or how a twin knows when their twin in another state is in trouble. Around here, with so many dogs being brought to me who are patients at the hospital, I get a ton of cases where the dogs tell me what's wrong with them, what treatment they need, and even when they're going to die. They're totally in tune with their bodies and what's happening in the world around them."

"Well, I hope you can get through to him for us," I said, trying to get things going. "Cody starts his radiation therapy tomorrow, and I want him to know that we're doing this to help him, and that I love him. I've got to go back to Texas for a week to deal with some job issues, but I'm coming back next weekend; I'm not going to leave him behind. I need him to know that, for once, I'm doing something for him and not worrying about my own problems. This is not about my job or my ego . . . it's about him."

"Let's see what we can do," Brenda said. She got down on her knees next to Cody as he sprawled out on the floor, closed her eyes, and held her hands over him. Immediately, he started inhaling in such a way that his chest was raising a good six inches with each breath, which, by itself, was already pretty amazing. I stole a look at Nancy and saw that her eyes were open wide in disbelief, but we both sat quietly. It seemed like an eternity, but it was in reality only about four or five minutes until Brenda opened her eyes and dropped her arms. Cody's breathing quickly returned to normal.

"Wow," she said. We waited for more.

"I feel bizarre telling you this," Brenda said. "I don't know your background, I don't know what you believe, but this is not a dog. This is a spirit guide in a dog's body."

"What's a spirit guide?" I asked.

"Well, some people might think of them as angels—they follow us around and sort of hang around up there in the subconscious and help us. My Catholic upbringing won't let me call them angels, because I think of angels as unattainable." She paused. "I knew it the moment I connected with Dakota—there was so much energy there, it was different from an ordinary animal. It really hit me, and I knew right away that he was a spirit guide."

Nancy and I weren't much help here. We didn't know what to say.

"I've come across spirit guides many times before," Brenda continued, "hanging around in the subconscious, but this is the first one that I've found actually residing in an animal or a human. I suspect that there could be others around, but this is the first time I've seen it in 13 years of doing this. Spirit guides are all around us, floating about—some people might call them guardian angels. They sometimes save your life and then disappear, but Dakota chose to take a physical form that was going to be here for a lifetime before moving on."

At that point, Nancy jumped in. "What's he doing here?"

"He's here to protect Mike and watch over him. Dakota is his guardian angel."

No one spoke for a moment while that sank in. Finally, Nancy broke the silence. "Where did he come from?"

"I asked him, and he said, 'I am not from this material world.' He sounds a little cocky to me, but I've heard that attitude before. Here on Earth, we're kind of lagging behind in the spiritual world."

"Why is he here as a dog?" I had to ask.

"He said he specifically came as a dog hoping to get people to see animals in different light, as spiritual beings. He wants to raise the status of animals in society, to show that they have consciousness, too, that they're more than dumb creatures. So in a sense, this dog has a larger purpose in mind, and he's using you to get his message across. He says that this is going to be hard for a lot of people, because in most religions, people have dominion over animals." Brenda took a deep breath. "I'm going back for more."

We witnessed the same scene once again, only this time it lasted a little longer. I'd never seen anything like it. Cody was taking in so much air that I thought he was going to raise up off the carpet. This time Brenda delivered our message to Dakota. He responded by telling her things that only he and I knew about, things I'd never even shared with Nancy.

"Dakota says that you need to stop worrying, that he knows that you love him. He wants you to stop worrying about him, and he doesn't want you to think about the same kind of stuff that you were thinking about that first night back in Dallas at the hotel."

I knew exactly what Brenda was talking about. Dakota and I had gone to Dallas to start work, and Nancy was going to join us later. The night before my first day back on the job, I was having some misgivings about going back to work, the move, and life in general, and in the hotel room, I spoke to Dakota about it. He'd never answered me . . . until now.

Brenda said that she found Dakota to be extremely down-to-earth, and based on his vibration, she felt that he'd been around for a long time in other forms. She called him a wise old soul.

Here are a few of the other thoughts that Cody shared with Brenda:

- He was fine with me going back to Texas for a few days and leaving him here. "Don't worry about me, just take care of yourself," he told me through Brenda.

- The treatment he was receiving at CSU was good and proper for his situation, and he liked the holistic approach.

- He didn't care if his body was cloned, but *he* wouldn't be there the next time around.

- As a young dog, he was neglected but not physically abused, and he'd ended up in a rescue situation because the family he was with just couldn't take care of him.

One very vivid memory came to my mind through all of this. The year before, Cody's Delta Society award was presented to him by Susan Chernak McElroy, author of the bestselling books *Animals As Teachers and Healers: True Stories and Reflections* and *Animals As Guides for the Soul: Stories of Life-Changing Encounters.* As she handed me his award, Susan had leaned over and whispered, "That's not a dog next to you. That's an angel by your side."

Until now, I'd always thought she was speaking somewhat figuratively . . . but now I knew differently.

■　■　■　■　■

CHAPTER TWELVE

Long-Distance Alert

Dakota told Brenda that his mission here on Earth was done. He said that he might hang around for another year or two, but he'd accomplished what he wanted to do. He didn't know what he'd be doing next, but it was nearly time for him to move on. We wondered what that meant. When the spirit guide decided to move on, would it just leave Cody's body behind? Or was he going to die?

Brenda couldn't answer that. "Very often, there are some unanswered questions from my sessions," she assured us. "I don't hold anything back from you—he just wouldn't get specific about this."

It was hard work listening to Dakota, and Nancy and I were exhausted from the evening's events. We knew what we saw, and we knew what we felt, but we didn't understand it, and that in itself took a lot out of us.

"I'm not sure if the world is ready to hear some of this stuff," Brenda admitted. "My clients often say to me, 'I'm a little scared of what you do, but I'm a little desperate.'"

"We're not desperate," I told her. "We just want to reassure him that we're doing what we think is best for him. We're not skeptics."

"Well, I don't worry too much about skeptics," she said. "I don't have the time to. I have too many clients whom I'm helping. If I worried about the skeptics, I wouldn't be able to do as much as I do for people and their animals. Dakota is kind of an isolated case for me. Usually I deal with dogs who tell me what's going wrong with them—but this is much different, way deeper."

"We heard a lot in what you said, a lot of things that we've seen or understood or felt, things that we've never talked about with anyone before," I said. "We were amazed at what you told us, not so much at what it was, but rather that you could get that information from him."

Brenda smiled. "A lot of people already think I'm crazy."

"That's okay," I told her. "A lot of people think I'm crazy, too."

It was very difficult to leave Dakota behind when we left for Plano the next day. The drive was very quiet. When Nancy and I did talk, we spoke about Cody. When we were silent, it was because we were thinking about him. We got home Sunday evening, and I immediately started planning to leave again. I wanted to get the week behind me as quickly as possible.

It was the first time in five years that Dakota and I had been more than a room apart. It's about 1,000 miles from Dallas to Fort Collins, Colorado, and I have to admit that I was afraid. What if I had another heart attack? Cody was supposed to be here to warn me, just as he had so many times over the past few years. I could fight through some of these lesser angina attacks, but if I had another major one, it would be over for me. But here I was thinking of my own health problems while Cody was fighting for his life, and that made me feel guilty for being so selfish. I wanted him to get well for his own sake, not mine. What he could do for me, when he was healthy again, would be plenty.

It wasn't easy to go home without Dakota, but there were things I had to take care of so that I could be with him for the rest of his treatment time. For instance, my cardiologist wanted to see me, and I had to take care of some things at work.

But as difficult as it was for me, this separation was even more trying for Nancy. I woke up more than once that week to find her sitting up in bed, looking at me, hugging Abbey, and crying softly. "I just worry that you aren't going to wake up," she told me the first night. "I'm doing my best here to fill in for Dakota."

At work, I could feel everyone watching me, even though they were trying to be subtle about it. It seemed as if there was always someone in my office, peering over the top of the partition, or calling to chat about nothing. It seemed as if they had held a secret meeting about me and were on some kind of schedule: "Whose turn is it to watch Lingenfelter?"

People stopped by for the "Dakota Report." After all, I wasn't the only one here who owed my life to Cody—he was family to my co-workers, too. It was pretty touching to see this response, and I knew that they were trying to make me feel better, but I'm not sure if it was helping me get through the separation or just making it tougher.

I spoke to Greg Ogilvie at least twice a day. The first day I called, Greg gave me the clinical report. It was a little early to see any measurable results from the ongoing work, but Greg's optimism and his belief in what they were doing made me feel good. The main treatment (radiation therapy) was proceeding in a state-of-the-art, high-tech fashion, a process which allowed it to target the tumor very specifically, in a way that minimized adverse effects on the heart and lungs. Other treatments included procedures that came directly from the ACC's research: Chemotherapy was undertaken, aimed at blocking certain enzymes that were part of cancer's attack on the body; and a special cancer diet, developed by Dr. Ogilvie, had been implemented. The cancer diet was high in complex carbohydrates, with certain high quality proteins and certain types of fats. The objective of the diet was to minimize the rapidly absorbed sugars that the cancer cells utilized for energy.

And since Dr. Ogilvie took him home each night, I knew that Dakota was getting plenty of personal attention, too. Greg may have been responsible for the dog during the day at the hospital, but his wife, Karla, and their 12-year-old daughter, Torrie, took charge of Dakota at home. They got help from their family dog, a 20-pound cockapoo named Cocoa. Cocoa and Cody had hit it off, Greg told me, and Greg was amazed that Cocoa had immediately accepted Dakota as if they were old friends. Greg said that Cocoa normally would bark and carry on when a new dog entered the house, but Cody was an exception from the beginning. The two dogs shared everything.

Cody had his green frog to keep him occupied. Greg told me that he'd been on the receiving end of that stuffed creature several times, but Torrie was usually Cody's target. In addition, Torrie had a great Beanie Baby collection in her room, which Dakota promptly discovered. He removed them to play with as his own, so Torrie started keeping her door closed. But that didn't last long, as Dakota soon learned how to open Torrie's door and got back into the Beanie Babies. With a smile, she put a sign on the door that read "No Dogs Allowed" and put a bungee cord on the door so that he couldn't get in when she wasn't there.

All in all (and even though I was 1,000 miles away), I liked the treatment Dakota was getting, and I was confident that his medical *and* nonmedical needs were being met.

■   ■   ■

Back in Dallas, it was Wednesday—Day Three without Dakota. I knew one thing that Cody wasn't missing: the Texas heat and humidity. I've never understood why they call them "the dog days of summer," when it's exactly the kind of weather that dogs hate. The air conditioning in the office had its moments, and this Wednesday was a doozy. It was always amazing to me that we had an office full of engineers, but no one understood how a thermostat worked.

My real purpose in coming back to work was to turn over my current project so that I could return to CSU for the next two weeks. Dave

Farley, Bill Sidoriak, and Rob Knoebber had been in my office for an hour, and at that point we were wrestling with the crucial executive decision of where to go to lunch. We'd been working the phones all morning, so when it rang this time, I hit the speaker button to answer, "This is Mike."

"Hi, Mike, it's Brenda McClelland."

I'd already spoken with Dr. Ogilvie earlier in the morning, so I was somewhat surprised to hear her voice. *Oh my God,* I thought, fearing the worst. *Dakota's dead.* "Hi, Brenda—what's going on?" I managed to choke out. "Is Dakota okay?"

"Yes, yes, yes, he's doing fine," she said. "Remember, he told you he'd be just fine, that you needed to worry about yourself, not him. So how are *you* doing, Mike?"

"Well, I'm not too bad," I told her. "I miss my angel, though, and I have my moments. Nancy found me crying in the bathroom this morning." I felt all the other eyes in the room on me. But these were good friends, and they already knew everything there was to know about Dakota and me.

"How's the heart?" Brenda asked, sounding like she was doing her doctor routine, working her way through the office exam.

"Other than the fact that you just jump-started it a little right there, I think that my heart's doing great," I said. "My doctors are right on top of things here; they even increased my medication yesterday."

"Okay, Mike, sit down."

Uh-oh, I thought. The guys in the room pulled a chair out for me and pushed me toward it. Dr. McClelland sensed my reaction and asked me if I was sitting down.

Now what? "Okay, I'm sitting down."

"Dakota is all right," she said. "I haven't seen him today, but he invaded my body a short time ago. I didn't invite him—in fact, I was working on some charts, and he just came to me out of nowhere. I could feel him all around me, so I allowed the contact. I said, 'What's wrong?' and he said, 'It's not me, it's Mike.' Dakota's worried about you, and he wanted me to get you a message."

That made me smile. I looked up and winked at Dave, Bill, and Rob. They'd heard my stories about Brenda's ability to communicate with Dakota, and now they were hearing a report about it firsthand over the speakerphone. They were transfixed.

"Dakota says that you have to lighten up or you're going to have a fatal heart attack," Brenda continued.

That kept me smiling: "'Lighten up?' Is that a pretty common spirit-guide expression?"

Brenda didn't skip a beat. "Well, that's what he said. He wants you to go find someone to drive you home now. And take your medication." I thought about this for a moment. I'd learned to put my faith in Dakota all these years, and I didn't question him then. Now, this was a little different, but I still had to put my faith in him—this time through Dr. McClelland.

I thought back on our meeting with Brenda in Colorado. Everything that she'd said and done had fallen right into place with everything we'd experienced, both before and after. I trusted her then, and I believed her when she told me what she was getting from Dakota. She showed me that she was for real, and that was good enough for me. I knew that it was also good enough for Bill, who had himself been saved by Dakota when Cody alerted on him in the office. And it was good enough for Dave and Rob, too, who were believers after being around Dakota and me throughout the years.

Dave was already on his feet, saying, "Come on, Mike. I'll drive you home."

Well, this was a first: a long-distance "alert" from Dakota. I took my medication on the way to the car to get a head start on anything that may have happened. By the time I got home, I was feeling tired; I thought that the medication had made me a little drowsy.

Nancy was at the front door to greet me, and when I related the story to her, she didn't question it at all. She just said, "Well, get in bed and try to get some rest."

About 45 minutes later, my chest felt like a huge weight had been dropped on it. The all-too-familiar signs of an angina attack were beginning to hit me, but the symptoms diminished fairly quickly. Its impact had been lessened, which was what usually happened when I took my medication in advance of an attack. I called Brenda that night to tell her about it.

"Mike, I debated how I would get this message to you," she said. "I was terrified to call you today. I'm a doctor, and you just don't call someone and tell them that they're going to have a heart attack—you might end up giving them one. So I decided I'd just call you and chat, to see how you were doing."

"What made you decide to tell me?"

"Well, when you told me about Nancy finding you crying in the bathroom this morning, that was the first push. Then when you told me about the doctor increasing your heart medication, that cinched it."

"Yes, but I told you that my doctor here had everything under control."

"But Mike, if everything was okay, he wouldn't have increased your medication," she told me. "You were telling me about the stress in your life, and I know that it wasn't easy for you to say those things in front of your colleagues. But after hearing about your concern for Dakota, I decided that I had to tell you what he told me."

"Well, I'm certainly glad that you did." So once again, I could thank Cody. He'd alerted on me many, many times in the past, and he'd managed to do it once again. Only this time, instead of pawing at me and jumping on me himself, he had an intermediary make a phone call. It was pretty amazing—I'd spent the last three years telling anyone who asked that Dakota alerted on me because he smelled the enzyme going from my heart to my brain.

Dogs do have superior olfactory senses compared to people, for they have something like 100 times as many olfactory cells as we do. But I really doubted that Dakota had smelled that enzyme from 1,000 miles away.

He really is my angel, I thought.

CHAPTER THIRTEEN

The Battle

I got back to Fort Collins after midnight that Saturday, so it was too late to get Dakota at Greg's. That night, I felt like a kid on Christmas Eve: I could hardly sleep as I counted the minutes until I was back together with Cody. At six o'clock the next morning, I met Greg at the clinic, where he was making his rounds. When Dakota came running up with the green frog in his mouth, I had a momentary flashback to the first time I'd seen it, five years before. I'd never been happier to have that silly thing shoved into my face. All I could think was, *Thank You, God.*

"He's been a great guest," Greg told me. "In fact, he's no longer a guest—he's a member of the family, and we hated to see him leave. We'll take him anytime you'd like us to. He longs to be around people every minute, so we did what we could to keep it that way."

Back at the hotel, it was nice to have some quiet time with Dakota. I'd missed him terribly, and I also wanted to thank him for his long-distance alert. When Cody and I arrived at the hospital the next morning, I was greeted by the staff like a long-lost member of the family, even though I'd only been gone for a week. I already felt like I'd lived there forever.

This time I wasn't going back to Texas without Dakota. I was going to stay for the final three weeks of his treatment program. So we got into the routine—radiation, chemotherapy, vitamins, diet, and acupuncture. Different facets of the therapy affected him differently: Some days he'd be up to playing ball in the local park; other days, especially when he had chemo, he just wanted to go home and sleep the rest of the day and night. But even on those days when he was worn out, he seemed happy. His tail was still going, and that frog was everywhere. We made lots of friends in the waiting room and around town. I'd talk about therapy animals, service dogs, CSU, and the bond that we have with our pets. Cody and I were still working, even 1,000 miles from home.

Dakota was truly a warrior. However, the battle that brought him here continued. He still had to beat the statistics in order to have a chance, and he still had a lot of things going against him. I remembered all the bad news that we'd had on our first visit here, but I kept thinking about the good news, too—that we'd caught the cancer fairly early and that we were at the best facility with the best doctor.

Greg had always been optimistic, and since *he* was, I was, too. His words kept coming back to me like a mantra: *"Life is a chain of moments that need to be celebrated."* So I made a point to celebrate every moment I had with Dakota. But I also believed that Greg was going to help us enjoy many more moments together.

Cancer isn't pretty. I thought back to that first x-ray, the one that had nearly dropped me to the floor, and I remembered how helpless and hopeless I'd felt. Then I thought about the second x-ray, which showed such improvement. I wanted to look forward to the next one, but I worried that the tumor seemed to be able to come and go so quickly.

"We're giving him what we know to be the best treatment available at this point in time," Greg told me. "We're adding a few new things on top of that standard of care, perhaps procedures that aren't yet proven, but it's nothing toxic."

Sometimes the days seemed really long—not so much because we were being put through a lot at the clinic, but rather because we just couldn't stay busy enough away from it. Our lives revolved around our time at the Animal Cancer Center, and when it was a short treatment day, or if the treatment took a lot out of Cody, there wasn't much to do other than sit around the hotel and read or watch TV. I talked to Nancy a couple of times a day, did a lot of phone updates for friends, and spent a lot of time on my laptop.

Occasionally, Dakota and I did get away, so we'd head up into the hills to Estes Park. The beauty of the snow-covered mountains, which teemed with elk, birds, and other wildlife, was a welcome physical and spiritual change from our usual environment in the hospital and the hotel. We'd drive around and take in the views, and I'd park the car and let Cody romp through the snow. It was good to see him playing, trying to decide what those elk were all about. I'd make snowballs and toss them in the air—sometimes he'd catch them, other times he'd just try to figure out what happened to them when they landed back in the snow.

We often just sat along the back roads and enjoyed each other's company. I spent a lot of time praying with Cody at my side, giving thanks to God for the time I'd had with him. But I'd also just hold him in my arms and wonder why God was allowing him to suffer. And so, even though these trips replenished us both, the ride back to CSU was always hard because I knew that Cody had to endure radiation again.

Our time here in Colorado was so very special that I decided that those mountains would become our final resting place. I left instructions with my family that when I died, I wanted to have my ashes mingled with Dakota's and spread up there. In this way, Dakota and I would be together forever.

■　　■　　■

Back in Fort Collins, we had another visit with Brenda McClelland. "He isn't listening well," I told her. "I know that sometimes the chemo takes a lot out of him, but he usually pays attention to me even when he doesn't feel very good."

Brenda sat over Dakota as she had before. He was very receptive; in fact, it appeared that he was fast asleep. Once Brenda closed her eyes and raised her hands over him (she calls it "hovering"), he started to inhale and expand his chest enormously, just like before.

Afterwards, Brenda said, "His energy is very low, and it's easy to understand why—it's the chemotherapy. Dakota told me that he's escaping from his body because he can't deal with it being sick. He says he's not dying, but spirit guides will leave their bodies before death because they can't stand the pain any longer."

She told me that because he didn't feel well, Dakota's chakra system was shutting down. She explained that the chakra system has its roots in Hinduism, and it's the source of spiritual power in the body. There are several of these centers in the body, and each is associated with a different Hindu god. These power centers run from the base of the spine to the top of the head, and will shut down in sick, elderly, or stressed animals or people, which results in lower energy levels.

"He says that he'll reconnect with the body after his chemo on Monday," Brenda said.

I corrected her. "His next chemo is tomorrow—Friday."

"Are you sure? He says it's Monday."

"No, it's tomorrow."

To end the session, Brenda gave Dakota a full-body Reiki . . . at his request. I thought it was a good session—I found out a little more from Cody, and he got reenergized from the Reiki. He seemed a little more alert that evening, but the next morning, he was still dragging a bit. After consulting with Greg, we decided to put off the chemotherapy until Monday. But hadn't Dakota told me that last night? How could he possibly have known that that was going to happen?

Greg was happy with Dakota's progress. We had a few more days to go at CSU, including one more visit with Brenda and one more chemotherapy treatment. I think that we were both going stir-crazy at the hotel. Cody had been acting more like his old self since his last Reiki session with Brenda. He was still somewhat lethargic, but not as bad as he was before. However, what bothered me was that he wasn't paying much attention to me, wouldn't always eat, and even chewed up one of his stuffed teddy bears, which was something he'd never done before. I told all this to Brenda when she arrived. She started with another Reiki session.

"Dakota had more energy in his body this time," she reported. "His chakra system wasn't completely shut down, and he's a little more tied to his body." He was calm at the end of the Reiki, and Brenda proceeded to communicate with him, just as she had before. "Good news," she said. "Dakota says that the cancer is gone."

"That's great. Any details?"

"No, he just says that it's gone, so it's time to go home."

"Is he mad at me?" I asked.

"No, but he really wants to get out of here," Brenda replied.

"How does he feel?"

"He's tired. He's not quite as cocky as he's been before."

"Well, I'm tired, too, and I don't have to go through nearly as much as he does. Tell him I'm ready to go home, too, and we will soon enough."

Then Brenda told me something rather startling: "He's prepared to go back to work for you, but he's ready to retire from all the travel. He says that it's time for you to start looking for a new dog."

"A new dog?" I wasn't sure that I'd heard her correctly. A new dog was the farthest thing from my mind at the moment.

"It's time to find someone to take his place. He told me that you'll find a golden retriever, which he says is the best breed, from rescue or from a breeder who's had one returned. It'll be six months old or so, and when you *do* find it, you'll know it's the right dog. Dakota will be here to help you train it."

"I'm not quite ready for that just yet," I said. "I want Dakota to be healthy and for us to be together for a long time."

I pondered what she'd said. A breeder of golden retrievers had told me the previous year that she'd help me find another service dog when the time came to replace Dakota. I don't think that either of us had thought that time would come quite so quickly, and I wasn't so sure that it was time to start looking anyway.

"Dakota says it's time," Brenda assured me. "He feels as if his job is done—remember, he told us that before. But he says that he's been able to get his message out, that he's helped make people aware that animals are capable of doing a lot more than they've been allowed to before. He says that he isn't the only one who can do this stuff. He's quite proud of himself; in fact, the last thing he said to me was, 'Look at what I can do, and I'm a dog.'"

I smiled at Brenda. "Well, he isn't going to get any argument from me on that one."

It was tough to sleep that night—with the very real possibility that Cody's cancer was gone, I was excited, scared, apprehensive, anxious—you name it. I wanted tomorrow to get here. I wanted to hear Dr. Ogilvie put what Dakota had told me into medical terms.

The next day, Greg and I had the chance to talk while we waited for Dakota's x-rays to process. "When we started on Dakota," he said, "we realized that he couldn't have any downtime. He lives each day to take care of you, and this cancer was impeding his ability to do that. He's your lifeline and part of your health and wellness. I think that he's ready to get back to his normal lifestyle—working with you and giving you and Nancy peace of mind. I'm optimistic that we're going to get good news here."

As if on cue, one of the staff brought in the x-rays. Greg put the first one on the light screen and stared for a moment. "Wow," he finally said. "Take a look, Mike. It's gone."

It *was* gone. And again, I thought back to that first x-ray. This was amazing—just a month ago I thought Dakota was facing his final days, but now the cancer had disappeared. It was unbelievable. Before I knew what was happening, the tears started to roll down my face.

Greg gave me a hug. "He's free of disease, Mike. The x-ray shows what the lab work has been showing. He's cancer free."

What could I say? Greg had given me back my angel . . . and he'd given me back my life. I kneeled down and embraced Dakota. "We're heading home, Code."

"Yes, it's time to get home, but you can't let up in the battle," Greg said. He told me that I shouldn't put Cody back to work right away because the cancer treatments had most likely compromised his immune system. Dakota was to continue with an anticancer regimen of chemotherapy once a week, along with additional medications.

"I'll have a letter for you later this afternoon, which will outline what we've found in your time here, and what needs to happen at home. I know that Dr. Krug is going to be happy for you and excited to be a continuing part of keeping Dakota healthy. We should never forget that his quick action at the beginning probably made the difference for Dakota here."

I believed that there were a lot of heroes out there for Dakota. The list started with Harold Krug and included Patty Neger, Marty Becker, and, of course, Greg and the people at ACC. How could we ever thank everyone? We needed to reach out to so many friends who had been an integral part of "Team Dakota" through their thoughts, e-mails, letters, and prayers. I wanted us to respond from the heart, so after we got home, this is the way Dakota did it (well, he had a little help) in an e-mail sent to friends:

From: Dakota Lingenfelter
To all my friends:
I have finished my radiation (15 exposures) at CSU and am
now into my 6th week of a 25-week chemo program. The orig-

inal tumor is gone, and there are no signs of cancer in my bone marrow. The lymph nodes may still have small cancer cells, so Dr. Greg Ogilvie at CSU is controlling it with chemo. I will go to CSU to be examined by Dr. Ogilvie and his staff (my cancer team) each month. I look forward to my visits at CSU; they are really very special people. Dr. Krug, my team member here in Plano, is giving me my chemo.

I know cancer is not a nice thing, but I have met many good and caring people because of it. I know that I will be a better partner for Mike due to this experience. We can both share our understanding of cancer with our old friends and the new ones we are still to meet. I have had unconditional love from everyone involved with my treatment, and I know that others who fear cancer can learn from my exposure to it. I am back working with my partner a couple of days a week. I enjoy this very much.

I thank each of you for your prayers and gifts. Please be assured that my family and I are grateful to each of you.

Love,
Dakota

Of course Dr. Ogilvie wanted to ensure Dakota's continuing recovery, so he sent Dr. Krug the following report and guide to follow-up work back in Texas:

Dear Dr. Krug:

Thank you for entrusting Dakota Lingenfelter to the Animal Cancer Center for anterior mediastinal [the area in front of the heart] *lymphoma and secondary hypercalcemia. Dakota and Mike are very special. We feel extraordinarily blessed to have had the opportunity to meet and get to know them.*

Our goals with Dakota have been to work hand in glove

with you and Mike to first determine the extent of the disease; second, to initiate therapy orchestrated to give Dakota the best chance for long term control of his cancer; and third, to minimize adverse effects.

The initial evaluation for Dakota's condition included a search for any evidence of cancer outside the primary mediastinal site. Findings were consistent with anterior mediastinal lymphoma without evidence of organ involvement one week after the initial Vincristine therapy. . . . We celebrated that victory with you and Mike . . . and then made plans how to maximize control of the tumor in the chest and then to attack the cancer that may be throughout his body in microscopic amounts.

The attack on Dakota's cancer consisted of radiation, chemotherapy, acupuncture, and osteopathic therapy, as well as routine, supportive care procedures. The radiation therapy was directed to the anterior mediastinal area.

The radiation therapy, delivered by one of the world's most advanced radiation therapy machines with three-dimensional radiation therapy planning, was delivered Monday through Friday, for a total of 15 fractions. Chest radiographs and cardiac ultrasonography taken toward the end of the third week confirmed that the chest was devoid of any evidence of the lymphoma, and there is no radiographic evidence of radiation damage to the lungs or heart at this time. The bottom line is that we were well on our way to controlling the cancer in the chest without significant damage to the lungs and heart at this time.

The next sword in this battle is chemotherapy. This drug therapy is designed to first help control the cancer in the chest, and second to help control the tumor cells elsewhere in the body.

Acupuncture and osteopathic therapy has been a mainstay

of therapy to minimize any discomfort, to maximize a sense of well-being, and to enhance the immune system.

Team Dakota should also look to the future. This future includes additional therapy to try to maximize control of the cancer using diet, radiation, and chemotherapy.

In summary, we look forward to working with you, Dakota, and Dakota's family as a member of "Team Dakota." We stand ready to help you in all ways to ensure that he does as well as possible. Know that a few prayers are being mixed in with all this medicine.

Warm regards,

Gregory K. Ogilvie, D.V.M.

■　　■　　■　　■　　■

CHAPTER FOURTEEN

Hope

Dakota was now a very special soul: He was a cancer survivor. His story could inspire others in their own battles with cancer, but he could also provide comfort to those who had loved ones (two- or four-legged) combatting the disease. So Greg Ogilvie invited us to share our story that summer at the Sky High Hope Camp, which is for children with cancer and their siblings. Located on an 880-acre ranch in Woodland Park, Colorado, near Pikes Peak, the camp is a project of the Ronald McDonald House Charities of Denver, Inc., and is supported by private and corporate donations and camper fees.

"Be a kid first and a patient second" is the motto for this camp, where physical changes such as limb loss, weight alterations, and hair loss, or the experience of having a sibling with cancer, are thought of as opportunities rather than limitations.

The campers, ranging in age from 8 to 16, take part in equestrian activities, arts and crafts, nature studies, water sports, volleyball, archery, and more. The camp is a wonderful, happy, heartstring-tugging place for kids who haven't had much of that in their lives. Greg and his CSU colleague, Dr. Stephen Withrow, have served as counselors and have helped oversee the camp events for about 20 years.

Greg asked me to bring Dakota as a very special guest, to serve a number of purposes: tennis-ball chaser; life raft; hug receiver; and most important, a source of hope, since he was a cancer survivor himself. The kids related to Dakota's story, and ended up getting some hope themselves: "Hey, *I* have lymphoma," they'd say, "and I'm getting better, too!"

Cody and the children seemed to give each other energy in a way that none of them had experienced for quite a while. The kids would throw tennis balls for Dakota to chase; they'd hang on to his tail as he swam around, or they'd climb with him on the rocks. When they rode horses, he'd run right along with them, and would sleep at their feet as they sat around the campfire. But more than anything, Cody was just there—to be petted by kids who were learning to use their arms again; to smile and wag his tail when kids who hadn't spoken for a while were ready to talk to him; to be a brace as someone struggled to get to their feet; to be hugged by someone who needed one. Dakota was in heaven.

This camp was everything that we'd ever done in animal-assisted therapy all rolled together and multiplied tenfold. It truly was the supreme example of unconditional love and acceptance. Dakota was like any dog—he didn't care if someone had lost their hair in chemotherapy or lost a limb to disease. Right before our eyes, Cody was giving a seminar on the impact of the human-animal bond. We saw how an animal could motivate, how an animal could help people forget their troubles, and how an animal could elicit a smile, stimulate conversation, evoke memories, and show what unconditional love was all about.

As I looked around the camp, I saw the smiles and the tears, I heard the laughter and the stories—and there was Dakota, right in the middle of everything. Whether he was just a golden retriever, a spirit guide sent from heaven, or something in between . . . Dakota had come to me for a reason, and my job was to share him with the world. Dakota had shown me everything the bond can and should be. After all we'd been through, I was a believer—and every day, Cody made other people believe, too.

■   ■   ■

After a wonderful week in the Rockies, Dakota and I drove to Fort Collins for our one-month checkup with Dr. Ogilvie. Walking up to the clinic, we ran into Brenda McClelland. I thought it was a nice coincidence to see her, as we weren't going to be here long and I hadn't let her know that we were coming. But someone else had told her—Brenda informed me that she'd heard from *Dakota* that his cancer was gone. She wanted to come by and see us both and wish us well, since she wasn't sure when she'd see us again.

Inside, Greg greeted us with a big smile. He was expecting the best, and so was I. I knew that Dakota was going to come out of this with flying colors. I knew it in my heart, but I also knew it because a certain four-legged angel had told me so!

Dr. Ogilvie did, indeed, declare Dakota cancer free. "There's no tumor, no cancer cells anywhere in the blood, nothing. We can't even find scar tissue in the x-ray." It couldn't have been better than that. "Our objective all along," Greg continued, "was to minimize Dakota's downtime during treatment and then return a healthy dog to you as soon as possible. But we can't let up—we need to continue the anticancer treatment regimen as standard maintenance."

Greg cupped Dakota's head in his hands and looked into his eyes as he spoke to me. "You've been empowered because of this dog, Mike. Dakota is very special to a lot of people—to you and Nancy, to Dr. Krug, to all of us here at CSU, to all of the kids and seniors that you visit, to everyone that you touch in your daily life. You are truly blessed. And I think that today, you understand the bond *and* the vibrancy and importance of life even more."

Greg and I embraced. I know that he knew what I was thinking, even though I didn't say it out loud: *I'll never be able to thank him enough for all that he's done for us.* I knew that the best way to try to express my gratitude would be to get out there and get back to what we were doing before all of this happened. So I vowed to do just that.

What a great drive home—we were back in Plano before we knew it. And as it turned out, I didn't have to wait long to test Dakota. The day after we got home, he and I were in the front yard, when he came up and started nuzzling me. I started looking for his ball, figuring that he was ready to be a real dog again, instead of a patient. But I didn't see his ball, and he kept nuzzling me. He finally pawed at me impatiently.

An alert! I went inside, took my medication, and went to bed. Dakota followed and lay down in front of me, his back up against my chest. After a few minutes, I felt the pain coming, but Cody was there for me again. I rode the attack out, almost happy to have the opportunity to do so.

I went back to work, but as Dr. Ogilvie instructed, I left Dakota at home. I missed him at the office, but the people there all understood my situation and probably watched me more than even Cody did. Of course, they wouldn't have been able to alert on me. But thankfully, I made it through the first week with little trouble. At first, Cody didn't seem to understand why he wasn't going with me. But by the end of the week, he wasn't quite as anxious when I left in the morning. (I think it helped that I took him out for a long walk each evening.)

The next week, I had to make a trip to Buffalo, and that was tougher on both of us. I had a couple of small angina episodes, but I was able to take my medication quickly enough to subdue the pain. Soon, Dakota regained enough of his strength to come back to work with me. Nancy said it wasn't soon enough for her—we were separately making her crazy instead of doing it together.

■　　■　　■

I decided to nominate Greg for the Delta Society Leo Bustad Companion Animal Veterinarian of the Year Award, which was named for Delta's co-founder. I received a wonderful e-mail from Greg after I told him what I'd done:

> *The biggest award or reward I can have is to know that you two are having extra days, weeks, months, and, if God is willing, years of extra time together. My prayer, my hope, is that I can make a difference in the lives of the people I touch and the animals that they bring. I am honored you would even think of forwarding my name for any award . . . but honestly, just to know that Dakota is feeling well and that you two are sharing days together that you would no longer have is an award beyond description.*
>
> *As you know, I knew Leo Bustad, and I was honored to be touched by his vision, friendship, and humor. . . . I believe that you and Dakota embody all that he had in mind to enrich the lives of animals and people through the bond. Your word on behalf of people and animals is worthy of the Leo Bustad Award. Therefore, being nominated by a far more deserving person is indeed humbling and an honor all its own.*

I think he was a little modest—how could anyone be more deserving than Greg Ogilvie?

It was also about this time that we got some more good news: Dakota had been selected for induction into the Texas Animal Hall of Fame, based on the nomination made by Dr. Harold Krug. The Hall of Fame is sponsored by the Texas Veterinary Medical Association (TVMA), and Dakota was selected "in recognition of his specialized service dog contributions."

In his nomination letter, Dr. Krug had written: "I've been in practice for 30 years and have never seen a dog with Dakota's obvious talents. He's just a well-trained, laid-back, easygoing puppy dog, which makes him perfect for what he does. Dakota and Mike's relationship is a dramatic example of the human-animal bond."

Dakota's plaque read as follows:

Texas Veterinary Medical Foundation
Texas Animal Hall of Fame
For Devotion To Mankind Through
Unselfish And Courageous Service
Dakota
Owned by: Michael Lingenfelter
Nominated by: Harold Krug, D.V.M. Dallas, Texas

Harold was thrilled for us, and we were honored that both he and the TVMA found Dakota worthy.

Things were going well—Dakota was getting stronger every day, and I was back at work. But suddenly there was a small bump in the road. Parsons Engineering, my longtime employer, informed me that they wanted to reassign me because of all my absences. That was certainly their prerogative, but it was nonetheless difficult to understand— the company had always been so supportive of me and had put up with so much for so long. But they'd apparently taken notice of exactly what my priorities were, which was something that I'd never tried to hide. The news wasn't all bad, though: Parsons wanted me to keep working as a part-time consultant. I could do this from home most of the time, with a little travel mixed in to oversee various projects around the country. I decided to accept the new duties.

It seemed that a lot of media were calling on us at this time—I think it was a continuing result of the Delta Society Beyond Limits Award, but also because of the story that aired on *Good Morning America*. The *American Kennel Club Gazette* produced a special "Dogs In Service to Mankind" issue (published in October 2000) with a nice feature on Dakota and a photo of us. There were a lot of our other Delta Society friends prominently featured in the issue, too. And the Discovery

Channel came to shoot a feature for its *Pet Love* show, and we were amused that they used a "stunt double" for Dakota—and for me! Their version of the story turned out to be slightly exaggerated, and Nancy and I laughingly agreed that the stunt doubles weren't nearly as good-looking as either Dakota or me! Later, we'd hear from Discovery that the on-line version of the story had generated nearly one million hits.

Now that I was no longer working at DART, Nancy and I had been talking about moving again. We gave a lot of thought to it, and decided to relocate to Huntsville, Alabama, where we could be near our daughter and grandchildren. Another attraction was the milder climate. I asked Greg Ogilvie and Marty Becker for recommendations for a veterinarian in the area, and they each had some suggestions, including the veterinary school at Auburn University. We moved in mid-December, and shortly after we got there, a couple of TV crews showed up. USA Network sent a crew to shoot a piece to air with its live telecast of the famous Westminster Kennel Club Dog Show from New York's Madison Square Garden in February. They told us later that it was one of the best features they'd ever had on the show, and they also made it available as streaming video on their Website.

The PAX Network came in about the same time and shot a feature that aired on its *Animal Miracles* show after the first of the year. They were so touched by the story that they promised to send a donation in Dakota's honor to the Animals Battling Cancer (ABC) Fund, a campaign to raise funds for facilities, equipment, programs, and staff at the Animal Cancer Center (ACC) at CSU. There were a number of beneficiaries of all of this attention to Dakota's story—ACC, Dr. Ogilvie and his great work, Delta Society, service dogs, animal-assisted therapy, and the human-animal bond. I was gratified that we could be a part of it all. This truly had become my life's mission.

Cody was very entertaining for the TV crews that came to our house. He'd romp around, play ball, and really do the golden-retriever routine for them. It was hard to believe that this was a dog that had been given only three months to live the previous May. To watch him, you couldn't have imagined that he'd even had cancer. He didn't look like he'd been sick a day in his life. That's why it was a little disappointing when Greg instructed us to keep him on maintenance chemotherapy for another three months. I felt so sorry for Dakota—it seemed as if every time he started to feel better, we'd just make him sick again.

■　　■　　■

I spent the next few months working on projects for Parsons, mostly the transportation system in Buffalo. Dakota and I were commuting to Buffalo for a couple of weeks each month, and I worked from home the rest of the time. We were certainly staying busy.

I continued to teach about ADA compliance occasionally—sometimes by invitation in a classroom setting and sometimes out of necessity "in the field." We were gradually teaching the Huntsville community about service-dog accessibility rights. It was still new to a lot of shop owners and building managers, as there were only five registered service dogs in the entire city. Most of the time, I was able to give the message in an educational, friendly way. People always wanted to interact with Dakota, and most would ask if it was okay to pet him. This usually gave me an opening to talk about service-dog etiquette: The dog is working and has to give all of his attention to his human partner. But having said that, I'd normally release Dakota and allow the individual to pet him, which presented the opportunity to continue the lessons about service dogs and the human-animal bond. It wasn't long before Dakota and I were pretty well known throughout the city.

Oddly enough, the very first trip we made out of the Huntsville Airport presented an accessibility situation for us. We checked in at the ticket counter for our flight without incident and headed for the gate. At the security checkpoint, two police officers stopped us and told me that dogs weren't allowed in the airport. I informed them that Dakota was a service dog, but they had no idea about the rules and guidelines regarding accessibility for such dogs. I spent a few minutes with them, showing them Dakota's ID card and certain sections of a handbook about rights for people with disabilities, and they politely let me continue to my gate, saying, "Sir, you have a nice day." Eventually, I used this as an entrée to schedule a formal ADA presentation to the Huntsville Police Department. The airlines were usually wonderful, and we actually often received special treatment from the gate agents or flight crews. I can't remember how many times we'd be told that the flight was full and that good seating would be a challenge—but inevitably, it would end up that the only empty seat on the airplane was the one next to us, giving Dakota the room he needed. I came to understand that this wasn't a coincidence.

That's not to say that everything always went smoothly. Occasionally we ran into someone who wasn't informed about accessibility laws, or worse, was *mis*informed. Once, I pulled out my cell phone and called the U.S. Attorney General's office so I could convince an overzealous gate agent that Dakota could indeed ride in the cabin with me. Another time, we put a phone call through to the president of the airline so that he could tell a gate agent what the policy (and the law) was. We got our seats.

One spring day, Cody and I were at the Newark airport, having just flown in from Huntsville for a fund-raising appearance for Delta Society. As we got to the front of the cab line, a driver refused to take us and wanted to take the next person in line. I wouldn't budge. The Port Authority Police got involved and pulled a few licenses until we got a driver to take us. On the same trip, we had a problem with a New York City taxi driver. That was really a bit of a surprise, as the New York Taxi & Limo Commission had had a serious problem a few years ago when a driver refused to pick up a woman with a service dog. They were hit with a lawsuit—rightfully so—and eventually settled out of court. But part of that settlement was to require sensitivity training for the drivers about the law regarding the rights of service dogs. Susan Duncan of Delta Society was involved in that settlement, and she was part of a big press event in New York announcing how this was now going to be part of the taxi culture in the city.

The finishing touch on the press event was that the cabs would all be furnished with stickers from Delta that said "Service Dogs Welcome," and these were to be prominently displayed on the exterior of the cabs. But any person with a service dog who's tried to catch a cab in New York City can tell you that, unfortunately, it's still a special challenge to get a driver to stop for you. And that's what happened to us. As a companion hailed the cab, I waited on the curb (Susan had told us that the reality in Manhattan was to keep the service dog out of sight). The cab stopped, and my friend opened the door for us. However, when Dakota and I came off the curb to get into the cab, the driver jumped out of the front seat and slammed the back door, waving his arms: "No dog, no dog!" I was angry and ready to challenge him, but cooler heads prevailed. We noted his medallion (license) number so we could report him. I was thankful that I didn't have to fight this battle every day in New York. How does someone with a service dog get around in this city? It seems nearly impossible—and this needs to be changed. Right after we were there, I heard a story about a woman with a hearing-assistance dog who was arrested on the subway when transit police wouldn't accept her explanation about her hidden disability and her service dog. So much for sensitivity training. (She filed suit, too.)

At a restaurant in Huntsville, the manager wanted to evict us, refusing to listen to an explanation. I was with a group of friends and was rather embarrassed about the situation. After the manager refused my suggestion that he call the police, I did. The responding officer had been at our presentation to his department, so he made short work of the visit, and the manager begrudgingly allowed us to stay. Because of the police report, the Justice Department later filed charges against the manager and the restaurant. I asked them to drop the charges after the manager promised to go through a training class.

Any of us with service dogs—whether we have hidden disabilities or very obvious ones—will tell whoever will listen that we're not interested in confrontations and lawsuits. We only want to be able to live our lives with dignity and to receive the same considerations as everyone else. We don't want to hold up a taxi line or a security point at the airport as we argue for our rights. That's embarrassing and belittling.

However, I'll never be the least bit hesitant to stand up for my rights, because I know that I'm standing up for all who come after me as well. I have the strength to do it, while others may not. Our dogs are a vital part of our lives, health, and well-being, and they can go wherever we can. I'm going to keep sharing that, cordially or forcefully, as long as I live.

■　　■　　■　　■　　■

CHAPTER FIFTEEN

The Student

In May 2001, Dakota and I headed back to CSU for his one-year checkup. We got a great report from Greg, and immediately let everyone know about it through this e-mail:

Hi Everyone:

It is with great pleasure that I send this e-mail today: It is Dakota's health and activity report after his first year of cancer treatment. Thanks to each of you in many different ways, I still have Dakota at my side after the first year of his cancer battle. He is still my best friend and guardian angel. He is still providing me with the protection I need to have and enjoy a free life without restrictions. His every step is still leading me in the direction of what God wants me to do with my life.

He is still touching people's hearts each and every day. His cancer is in remission, and his energy level is getting better each day. God has given each of you special talents, and I thank Him for directing me to each and every one of you. Each of us has had the special opportunity to know and love this Golden Angel sent to help me understand my purpose here on

Earth (I'm still learning each day).

Dakota is at my side, and I still cry thinking of the pain and suffering he's had with his cancer; and yet, each day I see his love for me and others. I see the hope that he brings to others as they hear his story—the hope they have is in getting their own Dakota (a full-time best friend). I know that we have a lot more work ahead of us, and with your help, Dakota will lead me to the next task. We are looking forward to going to Sky High Camp in Colorado again this year and seeing the kids enjoy Dakota, meeting new friends as we travel, and helping others gain insight in understanding there is hope for all of us. We just have to take the time to look and listen. Thank you each for your help.

> *Mike & Dakota*

Life was pretty good for us again. Dakota was healthy and happy, he was helping *me* stay healthy, we were getting more time with our family here in Huntsville, and we were working enough to stay challenged professionally and take care of our needs. Cody and I did have to spend a lot of time in Buffalo, as I was trying to get the project I was working on concluded. I was pushing myself pretty hard, and it was wearing me down. But I wanted to get this completed because there really wasn't anything else on the horizon for me that was pressing. That could always change, of course, but I thought that it would be nice if we could get this one over and done with.

One afternoon when we were in Buffalo, Dakota started coughing. It wasn't a harsh cough, it was more of a soft, trying-to-catch-his-breath kind of cough. I looked in his mouth to see if he was choking on something, but there was nothing in there. I led him over to his water bowl, and he drank a little. That helped for the moment, but the cough continued sporadically through the night and into the next day at the office. Lots of dogs cough, of course, but with his history, I was a little concerned and wanted to get him checked out as soon as possible. I called my travel agent and changed my flight so that I could get home that morning. I'm sure I could have found a vet in Buffalo, but I wanted to get him to someone I knew and trusted.

As we left the hotel, Cody seemed to have settled down a little bit. But when we got to the airport, he got sick again. He was having such trouble breathing that I had to practically carry him through the airport. He was gasping for air and using his stomach muscles to help him breathe. On the plane, I packed some ice in towels and covered him. He lay on the floor with his head on the seat next to me, and having his neck stretched out like that seemed to help his breathing. I got back to Huntsville late that afternoon and took him straight to our local veterinary clinic. They performed an EKG and took some x-rays immediately, noting that Dakota's heart was beating irregularly. The x-rays reflected a huge fluid buildup in his chest, and the vets worried about the potential of heart failure and pneumonia. They suggested that we take Cody to the vet school at Auburn University for some specialized attention.

Nancy and I called the school to tell them we were on our way, and we drove 200 miles to Auburn that night. We arrived at the hospital at midnight, and they went right to work. They drained three liters of fluid from Dakota's chest, and did an EKG to get under way. We went to our hotel at 2:30 A.M. and were the first ones through the hospital's doors at 7:00. The diagnosis was heart failure, and the doctors immediately put Dakota on heart drugs. But this didn't seem to be the answer, for after five days, Cody's condition hadn't changed.

We'd been in touch with Greg Ogilvie the entire time this was going on, and he was in constant consultation with the attending veterinarians. We finally decided to get Dakota back to his home-away-from-home at the Animal Cancer Center (ACC) at Colorado State University. We loaded him into the car and hit the road for Fort Collins, since we didn't think he could survive a flight. Just like he was on the airplane, Cody was packed in ice, and we drove with the air condition-ing set as cold as it could go.

Greg and his people at ACC were waiting for us at the end of our 1,500-mile drive. It didn't take long for them to turn things around for Dakota. Their diagnosis was arrhythmia, which was a result of the pres-sure on Cody's heart from the fluid buildup in his chest—and not from cardiac failure. They felt that the heart drugs were causing dehydration and kidney problems, and they seemed to be right about that because once Dakota was taken off those drugs, he got better in a hurry.

The treatment process took several days, and after things settled down a bit, we decided that once again we'd visit with Brenda McClelland. Cody greeted Brenda with a wagging tail. Even though he was a little tired from all that had gone on in the previous ten days, he was still happy to see his friends.

Brenda had another of her sessions with Dakota as Nancy and I again watched intently. Brenda was smiling when she finished. "He told me that's it—time for him to retire and for you to find a new dog to take his place," Brenda said. "He said that he'll try to lead you to the right dog to be able to handle this. He says that no one is going to do it as well as he does." We all smiled. Cody was still cocky—that had to be a good sign.

Brenda continued, "Dakota says he made this happen on purpose so he could convince you that it's time to retire, because he's getting tired of all the travel and life on the road. But he didn't mean for it to go this far, and he's worried that he can't reverse it. This backfired on him because now he has serious kidney damage. The good news is that he doesn't have any cancer or heart problems."

I had to ask: "Is he dying?"

"He told me that he isn't going to die yet, but he *is* serious about all of this. It's time to get another dog, Mike, because he isn't going to travel anymore. He said that he's already given you some ideas about the right dog."

I remembered what he told us before about an older puppy, a rescue dog, or a dog returned to a breeder. I also remembered that conversation I'd had two years before with a breeder who promised me a dog when Dakota was no longer able to work. I decided that it was time to call her.

But first we needed to get Dakota through this crisis. We were thrilled that he got so much better so quickly—Greg was going to have us expecting miracles from him all the time now. Cody wasn't totally recovered, but he was well on his way, so we decided that we could finish off his treatment at home. A day later, we were hugging Greg goodbye once again, and we were back on the road to Huntsville.

■   ■   ■

The morning after we got home, I sent an e-mail to Sophie Craighead, chairman of the board for Delta Society. Sophie's family had been breeding golden retrievers for many years, and she was the one who had told me that she'd find a dog for me when the time came. She didn't waste any time getting in touch with me—within hours of sending her the e-mail, my phone rang.

I told Sophie that I was looking for an older puppy, about six months of age, who had been returned for some reason.

"You know, Mike," she started, "we've been doing this a lot of years, and we've never had a dog returned to us."

I started thinking, *Oh, no, that isn't good news for me,* but Sophie wasn't finished. "That is, until this one," she continued. "We've gotten him back twice, but he just needs a chance and a loving home. I was so surprised to get him back again that I haven't been able to decide what to do with him. He's five months old, a nice and happy young dog. I've had a couple of people call me and try to buy him, but I wasn't sure if I was ready to let him go just yet. He's going to need a very special home because it just isn't fair to let him keep bouncing around." She paused for a moment. "But now I know why I kept him—it was because he was destined to be yours."

I didn't expect this to happen quite so fast. "I don't know what to say, Sophie."

"Don't say anything," she said. "I'm going to have Marjorie Moore, the breeder, talk to you about him."

"Where is this dog?" I asked.

"He's in Calgary."

"What's his name?"

"Harley. I don't know his registered name right off the top of my head."

"I want to pay you a fair price for him," I told her.

"Don't be silly. If you want him, he's yours."

"But— "

No buts, apparently. "I'll have Marjorie call you," Sophie interrupted. "I'll talk to you soon."

I'd hardly set the phone down when it rang again. Marjorie Moore was ready to tell me about Harley, so we visited for quite a while, and I hung up the phone thinking that this just might be the right dog. I shared that thought with Nancy, and she, as usual, was supportive.

A few minutes later, the phone rang yet again. Sophie wanted to know when I could go to Calgary. I told her I'd have to look into flights. "Can you go Sunday?" she asked.

"Well, I might be able to, but it depends on the fares and schedules."

"I'm going to have a ticket for you at the airport on Sunday morning. That will give you a day to get packed. My secretary will call you with the details."

"Let me give you a credit card number for the ticket," I said, reaching for my wallet.

"This is on me," she said.

"But—"

Once again, no buts. "I'm buying the ticket. Don't fight me on this one," she said. "You have a nice trip. It will be a first-class ticket, so you and Harley can have plenty of wiggle room when you come back."

At least I got two words out this time: "But, Sophie—"

"My secretary will call you shortly. Marjorie will pick you up at the airport."

Sophie's generosity is legendary in Delta Society circles, and now I was getting to see it firsthand. I related all of this to Nancy. "I sure hope this is the right dog," I said.

"Have you checked with Cody?"

"I was heading there next."

Dakota's eyes were turning bluish-gray, so I knew that he was listening to me. I told him about Harley, that I was concerned about bringing an untrained puppy on the airplane, and that I was worried about going to Canada without him to watch over me. I didn't need Brenda for this one—with those eyes, Dakota was once again letting me know that everything would be all right.

Marjorie was waiting outside customs in Calgary, and standing there next to her with his tail wagging was a little teddy bear named Harley. Marjorie told me that the plan was to go back to her farm to play with the little guy and meet his mom and dad. We put Harley in the backseat and headed out of the airport.

"I could use some lunch," Marjorie said. "Are you hungry?"

"Sure," I said. "Let's stop somewhere." I figured that if I could buy her lunch, at least I'd be contributing *something*. It wasn't long before we were pulling into the parking lot of a nice restaurant.

"I'll put Harley in his crate," she said.

"Wait a minute, Marjorie. This is as good a time as any to start his service-dog training," I told her. "I have a vest in my bag."

"Well, you know, he's not quite housebroken, and he's a little unruly at times. He hasn't had enough attention in his life, which is why he's been returned two different times."

"I think we'll be okay," I assured her. "I think Dakota will watch over us all."

Marjorie chuckled a little and said, "Why not?"

I put a service-dog vest on Harley, and we all went inside. Once we were seated, Harley went under the table and lay down on my foot and never moved, just like Dakota always did. That set the tone for the meal, and it was the perfect way for me to get into telling Marjorie some stories about Dakota's powers.

As we left, Marjorie said that she'd just witnessed a small miracle. I told her that if she hung around with us long enough, she'd see *more* than her share of miracles.

We had a great visit at Marjorie's, and Harley romped around like a typical puppy. His mother and father were friendly and outgoing, too. That night, we went out for dinner, and then Harley and I headed to the hotel. In spite of Marjorie's concerns about Harley's lack of training, he behaved like a fully trained service animal at dinner and in the hotel. Marjorie was in awe.

The next morning, Marjorie picked us up and took us to the airport. *This will certainly be an adventure,* I thought. To begin with, Harley had never been on an airplane, and we had a long flight back to Huntsville ahead of us. Marjorie wished us well, gave us each a hug, and shook her head in disbelief at the transformation of Harley in less than a day.

As Marjorie drove off, I looked down at Harley and said, "Dakota, I hope you told him everything."

He must have. My new friend made it through three airports and customs without a single problem. On the airplanes, Harley was a perfect gentleman, lying quietly at my feet and sleeping most of the way. Our entire trip could have been a service-dog training video. When we got home, I gave Dakota a big hug and thanked him.

Our first order of business was to give Harley a new name. It wasn't for any particular reason, like when Karen Costello renamed Dakota in order to signify a fresh start; rather, it was a way to honor one of our very favorite people. The puppy learned very quickly to answer to "Ogilvie." Nancy and I knew that his name would always provoke questions, which would give us the chance to speak about Dakota, CSU, and Greg. Ogilvie quickly became a very special part of our family, readily accepted by Abbey and Dakota. However, some toys were still off-limits to him, particularly Dakota's stuffed teddy bears. His house-training was over quickly—after two accidents the first day, he never had another. He learned to follow the big dogs to the garage and how to get into the car with only a little bit of help from us. Ogilvie also got into our daily routine around town without much trauma. He loved his car rides, as well as going to new places. In his first week, he visited the barber shop, the bank, a restaurant, and the veterinarian's office to get his shots. He also got licensed as a service dog in training in the state of Alabama.

Dakota never took another business trip with me. For the rest of the summer, he was mostly "just" a dog, hanging out in the yard, enjoying life, and watching the ducks, geese, and herons that congregated near our house. He played with Abbey constantly, and also found time for Ogilvie—some of it was play, and some was posturing to set appropriate boundaries between the mentor and his apprentice.

■　　■　　■

I'd been thinking about the kids and the peaceful, healing experience of the Sky High Hope Cancer Camp nearly every day since we were there the previous summer, so when Greg called to invite Dakota and me to this year's camp, there was no hesitation in accepting. I knew that Cody would want to be there, and so did I. It would be good for us both, but most important, we could once again help some kids in need.

The timing of our last visit, coming right after a positive checkup at the Animal Cancer Center, helped to make it very special—we were in exactly the right frame of mind to help those kids. And now, after a few challenges for Dakota this year, things were going well once again. He was healthy and happy, and we were ready to go back. I'd kept my promise to Dakota to allow him to retire, and he seemed to be enjoying it. However, there were times when he'd follow me around the house as I was packing to go on a business trip, and I'd wonder if he was trying to tell me something. This time, as I packed for camp, he left no doubt in my mind. My suitcase was open on the bed, and I was putting something in it when he came up with his green frog in his mouth. It was as if he were saying, "I'm coming, too." Somehow, he knew that this trip was to be something different. I'd promised Dakota that I would never put him on an airplane again, so we were going to drive the 1,500 miles to Colorado. This long road trip would give us some quiet time together, just the two of us. It was something that we hadn't had for a while.

Saturday was our first day on the road. It was a nice start to the trip—the roads weren't too crowded and the weather was wonderful as we made our way into Kentucky. It was still daylight when we stopped at our hotel for the night, so we found a park and played a little ball. Cody seemed to run out of gas, so we headed back to the hotel. "We've got a long trip in front of us, Code," I told him. "There's going to be lots of playing ball in Colorado, so I'm glad you're pacing yourself."

Sunday was another great advertisement for seeing the USA by automobile. I gave Dakota a little boost into the backseat, knowing full well that he'd be up in the passenger's seat as soon as he decided he wanted to be. But as we neared the Illinois border, Cody was still in the back. And then I heard the sound I'd hoped to never hear again—the same cough he'd started in Buffalo, the cough that took us from Auburn to CSU to Huntsville, and eventually to Calgary.

I nearly drove off the road. There was no doubt in my mind what this was. Greg had said that it could recur, but I guess I'd gotten a little complacent over the past few weeks when Dakota hadn't shown any problems. But now, I knew that we weren't going anywhere until we saw a veterinarian. The trouble was, we were in a strange town on a

Sunday morning—not exactly ideal circumstances for driving up to the local vet. I didn't even know the name of the town we were in, but it was large enough to have an emergency vet listed in the phone book. I called the number and got an answering service. I drove to the clinic, taking a chance that there might be someone there, only to discover an empty parking lot and a locked door.

I sat in the Jeep, comforting Cody and struggling to make a decision. Did I drive on and try to find a vet on the way to the camp? Or did I head home? Either way, I really didn't like the idea of being on the road when Dakota needed attention. I thought about getting back to see Greg, but he was at the Cancer Camp all week, not at CSU. I dialed his cell-phone number and left him a message, hoping that he'd be able to get back to me quickly.

We were only about 500 miles from Huntsville, as opposed to 1,000 to Colorado Springs—that was a deciding factor. I called Nancy and told her we were coming home. "It sounds like the same cough as in Buffalo," I told her. "He seemed fine yesterday when we were playing in the park. Maybe he's getting fluid in there again, like Greg told us could happen."

"Come on home," Nancy said.

We were on our way. Twice more, I tried to find a veterinarian, but had the same experience I'd had before. If it said "24-Hour Emergency Service" in the phone book, then where were these people? I was angry enough to think about kicking in a door or two.

Dakota wasn't struggling quite as much as he'd been in Buffalo, but I didn't want to waste any time. By the time Greg called me back from Cancer Camp that afternoon, we were well our the way back to Alabama. "Let's not jump to any conclusions, here," he said. "With his history, we need to be looking for a number of things."

We got back home in a hurry and brought Cody right to our local vet. Under Greg's direction from Colorado, we found that there still was no evidence of cancer. That was a relief, but there was still fluid leaking into Dakota's chest, just as there had been nearly two months before. A little more than three liters of fluid was drained from Dakota's chest the first week in August. At that point in time, the vet started to send both blood and urine samples to CSU every week. I wanted Greg involved as much as possible, and he was continuing to lead the treatment from afar. For the next two months, that much fluid was drained from him every three weeks.

The first week in October, Cody and I made a presentation to the Academy for Lifetime Learning at the University of Alabama in Huntsville about service dogs and the ADA. As usual, Dakota was a big hit as we delivered our messages about health, science, spirituality, and the human-animal bond. Cody was a trooper—even though he was having a catheter stuck in his chest every couple of weeks, he gave no sign of being anything less than a loving, happy golden retriever and loyal service dog.

But right about this time, the interval between his treatments suddenly got shorter. The fluid was building up faster and faster. They were still draining three liters of fluid at a time from him, but it was happening every ten days, and then every week. It had been almost exactly five months since his checkup at the Animal Cancer Center found him cancer free. But it was time to get him back to ACC once again.

Nancy, Ogilvie, Dakota, and I were soon on the road again.

■　　■　　■　　■　　■

CHAPTER SIXTEEN

Looking for Another Miracle

Of course I knew that Dakota couldn't live forever, but I wanted him to at least live *longer*. I wanted him to get well and for his suffering to stop, but the questions haunted me: Could I help him one more time? Was he going to get yet another medical miracle from Greg Ogilvie, or could Brenda McClelland help us find another spiritual one? Did Cody even *have* another miracle left in him?

I was trying to remain hopeful, but I was afraid that we might be out of options. I didn't want to think about that. I wanted answers—I thought that there were some to be had, but I was afraid of what they might be. I thought back to when I'd gone to my cardiologist after my surgeries several years before, when I'd demanded answers but got nothing but bad news. I didn't want that to happen here. Yet, in spite of the reality, I was trying to be optimistic.

A lot of different feelings came about on the journey back to Fort Collins. The contrast between hope and fear drove them all. I *really* wanted to be hopeful and keep the faith. I'd kept the faith ever since Greg had given me his first pep talk, and I knew that if there was something good that could happen, he would make it happen. But the truth

155

was that I was really afraid that there might be only one way for Dakota to find peace.

Whether it was fear or hope that was guiding us, this trip was slightly cathartic. The long drive gave Nancy and me time with Cody and with each other. We needed both. Nancy has always been a rock for me, and this time was no different. For as much as Dakota had given me in his life, none of it would have been possible or meaningful without Nancy. Every minute of the trip, like every moment I had with Cody, was special. I'd learned a lot from him. He was a great teacher, and one of the most important things he taught me was to live for the moment, which was what we were doing on this trip. Nancy and I hoped that we'd hear good news from Greg, but we also prayed for the strength to deal with bad news.

Dakota's chest had been drained the Saturday morning before we left Huntsville in order to help his comfort level on the trip. He didn't have any problems on the journey—he romped with Ogilvie at the rest stops and didn't cough at all.

Ogilvie seemed to sense that something significant was going on. He paid a lot of attention to Cody, and, for a change, it wasn't in the pestering-puppy way. He nuzzled Dakota, pawed at him playfully and gently, and lay down next to Cody with his head on his chest. It was evident that Ogilvie was getting more and more confident about his relationship with Dakota, even more quickly than he was at home. It seemed to me that Ogilvie knew that he was the heir apparent, and he was feeling his way into the role while still trying to be respectful of Cody. I could see that Ogilvie was growing up on this trip, and I hoped that it was because he was paying attention to whatever it was that his teacher was sharing with him.

It was reassuring to be going back to the Animal Cancer Center (ACC), where we were certain that Greg and his people would have the answers, and where we knew that Dakota was at home. We arrived in Fort Collins late Sunday night. Dakota and Ogilvie were a little weary from all the driving—as were Nancy and I. We went straight to bed, as we had a big day in front of us.

■   ■   ■

When we got to ACC on Monday morning, Greg was waiting for us at the door with a list of things he and his staff were going to do. They got right to it—draining the fluid from Cody's chest and collecting blood for lab work, then ultrasound and x-rays. The good news from all of this was that there wasn't any sign of cancer, or involvement of the heart or lungs. The bad news was that there wasn't anything definitive in those results that could tell us where the fluid was coming from.

Dakota had beaten cancer—what could be worse than that?

"It just doesn't seem fair," Greg told us. "We all worked so hard to get rid of the cancer, and when he was cured, we rejoiced. It really hurts to have something else come in here and create problems."

Greg said that the results from one of the tests wouldn't be in until the next afternoon and that there wasn't really anything for us to do until then. He said that he'd talk to us about options on how we might proceed. I could tell that Greg, like all of us, was a little frustrated. He was always pretty good about staying positive and upbeat, but for the first time, I could tell that he was down. After all, this dog had been a member of his family, both at ACC and in his own home . . . Greg was hurting, too.

That night at the hotel, we decided to make the next day "Dakota's Day." Fueled by our memories of the Sky High Hope Camp, we announced that it was time once again to "be a dog first and a patient second." So that morning Nancy and I dropped Ogilvie off at the groomer, and we headed to the foothills with Cody for some special playtime for just the three of us. And special it was—we thoroughly enjoyed our day together. Dakota walked and ran in the fields as if God was with him. He had a presence that was majestic, commanding, and imposing. Nancy and I could feel his spirit as he romped and played with us, and we tried to capture every minute we still had with him by taking dozens of photographs.

As I watched my angel, the flashbacks were beginning. I thought about him being chained up in someone's backyard . . . about little Linda at the Shriners Hospital, Annette at the nursing home, my colleagues at work being saved by his alerting skills, and the engineer that committed suicide in Buffalo . . . about that x-ray at Dr. Krug's . . . about all the wonderful people at CSU. . . . *Please, God, can't we get him through this?* I prayed. *Can't we collect a few more memories?*

I wished that the afternoon would never end, but it was time to pick up Ogilvie and head for the ACC. When we got there, we found out that the latest lab work still didn't show anything, and Greg told us that we were down to our final choices to continue the quest for answers. The first would be to insert a catheter into Dakota's heart to measure pressures. The second alternative was to insert an endoscope into his chest to look for damage and sources of trouble. If neither of these procedures proved helpful, then exploratory surgery might be the last hope to answer some questions.

"One last option might be to put a catheter in his chest to allow for drainage of that fluid. You could take him home with you and deal with it that way for as long as he's comfortable, but chances are you're talking about a few weeks at most." That didn't sound too appealing—Cody had lived with dignity through a lot of things in his life, and I wanted to preserve that dignity for him.

"Why don't you go back to the hotel tonight and think about it?" Greg suggested. "We can go into his chest tomorrow morning with the catheter and the scope and try to determine exactly what's going on in there. If it's something we can deal with, we will—but if it isn't, you may have to make some difficult decisions on the spot."

I told Greg that I'd be ready to consider the options as they arose.

The surgery was scheduled for the next morning at seven, so we headed back to the hotel. I was afraid that we were running out of miracles. I called Brenda McClelland and made arrangements for her to meet us at the hotel later that evening. We had some spare time, so Dakota and I left Nancy and Ogilvie at the hotel and went down the road to the dog groomer. I wanted him to look good for everyone.

I'd told Brenda that Cody had just been through some more tests, and when she got there that night, she knew that we were troubled. I asked her if she'd find out what Dakota could tell us about his health. I also asked that she tell him that I loved him and wanted to do what was right for him.

Nancy and I had seen it happen a few times now, but we were still enthralled (as was Ogilvie) as we watched Brenda hover over Cody with her eyes shut and her arms raised as she communicated with him. Once again, his chest expanded at least six inches and looked like an overfilled balloon, even as he lay peacefully asleep.

As she disconnected from the session, Brenda looked concerned. "He's regretting that his health is failing so quickly—that was never his intention," she reported. "But he said that it's his entire chest, not his heart or his lungs, and that it isn't cancer or related to the radiation treatments."

Dakota got to his feet and came over to sit down in front of me. I was stroking his head in my lap. "Is he dying?" I asked.

"No, not by his definition. He says he's getting ready to leave, but he's not dying." Brenda paused and seemed to be trying to find the words. "He didn't indicate whether he'd be back. He kind of feels that his work is done here. He's taught you a lot, and you've helped him show people everywhere just what animals can do for them. He said to tell you not to worry. You're going to be okay—he'll see to that."

I was afraid to ask the next question: "Did you tell him that I'm not ready to let him go?"

"I did," Brenda answered, "and he told me that he isn't particularly ready to die yet himself, but everything's leaking in his chest and it's gone beyond his control."

I was fighting back the tears. "What if . . . " I couldn't finish the question; instead, I hugged Cody.

"He says that if you need to euthanize him, he's okay with that," Brenda said.

There was no more holding back now: As I'd done many times before, I held my angel close and sobbed uncontrollably.

■   ■   ▓

Nancy and I knew that the end was near, and we wept all night long. Dakota just lay quietly on the bed between us, allowing us to hold and love him. And as he'd done his entire life, he returned the love by kissing us and staying with us.

I didn't want Wednesday to come, but it did, and that morning we walked slowly in to the ACC. There were a lot of people waiting for us, including staff, students, and administrators—and, as usual, Greg was there to greet us at the door, giving each of us a big hug. I'm sure it wasn't too difficult to tell that we'd all experienced a rough night.

The morning wasn't going much better, as Nancy and I were both anticipating the worst. We'd discussed some options ourselves earlier and decided on a couple of things: First, if Greg didn't find anything with the catheter or the endoscope, and if the long-term outlook wasn't any different than the scenario he presented yesterday, we'd ask him to forego exploratory surgery and euthanize Cody before he came out of anesthesia. And second, we wanted the ACC to perform a full autopsy, not just for us, but for themselves, the students, and future patients. This was a teaching hospital, after all, and maybe Dakota's legacy could be to help save another dog's life someday. Or perhaps he could even provide some bit of progress in the fight against cancer and eventually save human lives, too.

"Are you ready?" Greg said softly.

I didn't answer. I bent over, hugged Dakota and gave him a kiss, as did Nancy. I handed Greg the leash, and he bent over and petted Cody, too. He then handed the leash to one of his students, who walked away with Dakota as Greg stayed with us.

Cody turned his head over his shoulder to look at us as he was led down that hallway. He was hesitating slightly, and I think he was trying to say good-bye to us with his eyes. I'll always remember this. I couldn't believe that it could very well be the last time that I was going to look into those eyes, which had said so much to me over the years.

The wait was excruciating, but we had lots of company, and that helped. Tamina Toray and Teri Nelsen, the director and assistant director of the Argus Family Support Services, were there with us the entire time. Dr. Stephen Withrow, Greg's colleague who helped out with the Sky High Hope Camp, stopped by several times, and his administrative assistant, Linda Reed, was also there with Nancy and me.

Greg came out a little after 9 A.M. He got right to the point, saying, "Mike, there's nothing we can do." That didn't surprise any of us: It was pretty evident that this was the expected outcome, judging from the show of support from everyone.

Greg went on to report that the catheter in Dakota's heart had shown normal pressure on both sides. The endoscopy showed that everything was red in the chest wall, but with all of the ongoing activity, that was to be expected. The scope wasn't conclusive, and it really didn't tell us anything that we didn't already know or suspect.

He went on to tell us that exploratory surgery may or may not have been able give us some other ideas, but he really didn't think it would. "I'll be honest," Greg said. "We can open up his chest and go in there and look around, but I don't think we're going to get any answers that we don't already have. That fluid seems to be coming from the chest wall itself, and even if we find out exactly where it's coming from, chances are pretty slim that we'd be able to do anything about it. It's probably coming from his blood vessels or lymphatics, or maybe both."

"That's only going to hurt him more," I said. "My chest has been cut open a couple of times, and I know how bad that hurt me. I'm not putting him through that." There was silence all around. I'd just eliminated the last option.

"I think you're doing the right thing," Greg said. The silence continued, broken only by the soft sobbing of several people, including Nancy and me. "He's still under anesthesia," Greg said. "Do you want to come back and say good-bye?"

I told him that I didn't think I could do that.

"How about if we bring him up on the gurney to the Family Support Services room?" This would allow Tamina and Teri to help us during the final difficult moments, so I agreed to that.

When Cody was brought into the room, Greg suggested that they take him off the gurney and put him on a mat on the floor so I could hold him while they administered the euthanasia injection.

But through my tears, I said, "I can't watch him die."

Nancy and I said our good-byes to Dakota and went outside to wait for the final word. It didn't take long. As soon as it was over, Greg came out to get us and we went back in for one last time with Cody.

"He went peacefully," Greg reported. "No movement, no noise."

I picked up Dakota's foot, and it was already eerily cold. I leaned over, gave him a hug and a kiss, and whispered into his ear, "I'll see you soon." Nancy whispered something to him, too, and we each clipped a lock of his hair.

Greg was holding his composure, but I know that he was frustrated at not being able to win this last battle for us. And I know that he was hurting as badly as we were. He quietly promised that he'd take care of Cody's cremation and send us his ashes. We worked our way to the door and through the waiting room, hugging and kissing everyone as we went, promising to keep in touch. We wanted out of there quickly.

I felt that *my* life had ended, too. I was angry at God, and I have to admit that I momentarily lost my faith. I couldn't understand how God could make Dakota suffer so badly when he'd only done good things his entire life. And I'll never understand why God took him before he took me. Cody taught me how to live, and he made me *want* to live— now he was gone, and I wanted to die. *Why should I go on?* I thought. I was back to wanting to end it all.

"Dakota worked hard to bring you back," Nancy was quick to respond. "You have so much in your life now because of him. This kind of talk is *not* what he would want. You pick yourself up and get going again."

She was right. After we collected ourselves, we had brief telephone conversations with our children to fill them in on the final events. Our grandson Brad, who was at our home in Huntsville watching over Nancy's father, said that he suspected the worst when Abbey uncharacteristically started acting anxious and agitated on Wednesday morning. Amazingly, Brad didn't even find out about Cody's death until that afternoon. There was no doubt in my mind that Dakota had paid Abbey one final visit.

I don't remember too much about the trip home from Colorado. Putting Cody down was the hardest thing I'd ever done. I spent much of the drive wiping away my tears, and Nancy and I could barely speak to one another. As we motored down the road, I remembered every single place we'd stopped with Dakota. I couldn't believe he was gone. I felt so alone and helpless, and I was having trouble understanding why God had let this happen.

After we got home, I went on the Internet and found a book called *Doctors Cry, Too: Essays from the Heart of a Physician,* by Frank H. Boehm, M.D., which deals with the compassion that's needed in order to be a good doctor. I ordered it for Greg and sent it to him on behalf of Cody.

Greg called several times over the next few weeks, as a friend to talk from the heart, and as a doctor to fill us in on the final findings. He said that, after reviewing all of the tests and lab work and the autopsy, his opinion was that the fluid accumulation in Dakota's chest wasn't related to either the cancer itself or the treatment.

In the weeks following Cody's passing, the people from the Argus Family Support Group were compassionate and caring, which was something that we'd come to expect from them (and everyone else at CSU). Teri and Tamina offered me their encouragement and guidance by phone and e-mail on a daily basis—they knew that I was on the edge, and they even found a counselor for me to see in Huntsville.

■　　■　　■

I'll never get over losing Dakota, and I don't want to. But I *have* learned to cope with losing him as I think about the wonderful life we had together and all the great lessons he taught me and everyone else he touched.

I still get up every day and touch the little gold angel that's pinned to the sun visor of our Jeep. I say, "Thank you, Dakota. Thanks for your love and for giving me my life again."

In the end, Cody's greatest lesson—the one all-encompassing physical, spiritual, and mental message about what his time here with me was all about—came from him through Brenda.

"You need to be aware of your world," she shared. "He says that just because he tells you to take your medication, that doesn't mean that you're going to live. *You* have to put something into it, too."

Thank you, Dakota.

■　　■　　■　　■　　■

CHAPTER SEVENTEEN

Dakota's Legacy

Do not stand at my grave and weep;
I am not there, I do not sleep.
I am a thousand winds that blow,
I am the diamond glints on snow.
I am the sunlight on ripened grain,
I am the gentle autumn's rain.
When you awaken in the morning's hush,
I am the swift uplifting rush
Of quiet birds in circled flight.
I am the soft stars that shine at night.
Do not stand at my grave and cry;
I am not there, I did not die.

— Native American Prayer

In 1994, when my doctors told me that a dog could help me get well, both mentally and physically, I thought they were crazy. I had health problems that weren't going to magically disappear, and I didn't want to continue to live each day just waiting for that final and inevitable heart attack. What good would a dog do me?

If I'd had my way after that first day I spent with Dakota, he would have gone back to being someone else's problem instead of mine. He would have been back in a crate in someone's kitchen, or chained up again in someone's backyard . . . or worse. He was a rescue dog, after all—no one wanted him, and at that point, neither did I.

But instead, for some reason he stayed. Maybe it was the green frog. Maybe it was because Nancy's observation ("He's just like you") created a place for him in my life and in my heart. Maybe it was simply destiny.

Or, maybe it was those eyes that looked into my soul and helped me be at peace. Dakota's eyes would comfort me for hours at a time with intuitive communication—they'd tell me I was going to be okay, that things would work out, and that I still had more to contribute to the world. Cody's eyes melted people and controlled them with the classic "Dakota look":

> Dear Mr. Lingenfelter,
> It was so wonderful meeting you and Dakota on my flight to Buffalo. The woman who was seated next to you grabbed my arm and said, "I wish I could explain it to you—I wish I could tell you what I saw in that dog's eyes." She said it was like nothing else she had ever felt before. Then, as we were deplaning, after I said good-bye to you and Dakota, another woman stopped me and said, "I don't mean to pry, but I have to know about that dog . . . I can't explain, but there was 'something' about him." I told her briefly, and she said she knew . . . she said she could tell when she looked in Dakota's eyes.
> As I told you, I don't talk about my dad's death with just anyone. Only a very few people know what I'm about to tell you about "Thumper." That little dog saved my dad's life for those

extra years . . . I thought I would die when I had to put Thumper to sleep (he was 18). I picked him up with my dad when I was 15 years old, Daddy had to have <u>him</u>, not the white one I wanted-ed. I always got everything I wanted, but for some reason, Dad had to have <u>him</u>.

Thumper licked my tears away every night while I was systematically trying very hard to kill myself. He never left my side and he stayed with me until I was 33 years old and had my son, whom I named Michael, after my dad . . . I connected on an unexplainable level with this little being. I believe Dakota is <u>your</u> angel, like Thumper was mine.

After Daddy died, Thumper's eyes looked so sad. It wasn't my imagination—the expression in his eyes had changed. I know I am alive today because of his gifts, like the ones Dakota had. There is a reason "dog" is "God" backwards—it's the closest thing to God's love.

I want to thank Dakota for touching my heart. I'm so glad I was working that flight. I will never forget you both.

Take care and God bless,

Taffy (Flight Attendant)

Cody had many gifts, but foremost was his ability to share unconditional love with everyone he met. Touching him could make fear and pain go away:

Hello Mike,

A while ago, I met you and Dakota at the front desk of the hotel where I worked. I saw he was a beautiful creation, and I had to come over and pet him. At that time, I didn't know of his remarkable gifts—I just felt a great sense of peace and calm when I petted him. I never forgot him nor you. What a remarkable story you told us.

Last spring, I once again had the pleasure to see you and Dakota at the hotel, and I remember that I knelt down and hugged Dakota. What a feeling!!! I was walking upstairs to my office, and I thought, Oh, my—I have just hugged an angel!

What a gift you have been given. I have talked to many friends and occasionally our discussions talk of God and angels . . . I can say with great honor and humility that I have indeed been hugged by an angel.

Blessings,

Joyce

Dakota showed me how to live my life. He took me to schools, to kids with special needs, to Sky High Hope Camp, to nursing homes, and into situations where we were clearing the way for people with disabilities. He showed me so much, and I continue to live my life that way, every day, because of him. But clearly I wasn't the only one who benefited from what he taught:

The second grade teachers and students at Foot of Ten Elementary School would like to write a letter to the Delta Society, acknowledging the excellent educational presentations of Mr. Michael Lingenfelter of Duncansville, PA. Mr. Lingenfelter and his service dog, Dakota, have visited our school for the last several years.

Using Dakota as a perfect service dog model, Mr. Lingenfelter described his serious medical condition and his close relationship to Dakota. Dakota's service dog responsibilities were discussed at length. Mr. Lingenfelter taught all of us about the importance of service dogs in our ever-changing society. He also reinforced the need for the close human/animal bonds in all our lives. His work should be recognized and commended.

Very sincerely,

Second Grade Teachers, Foot of Ten Elementary School

■   ■   ■

Dakota gave me what I needed to recover from my depression—understanding and purpose in life. He challenged me to go forward and present his gifts to the world. When I accepted his challenge, he provided me with the protection that I needed to get back into society by forewarning me of the onset of my angina attacks. He showed me how to use him to help others, and how to heal myself with his love.

When I went back to work, he controlled my environment so that I wouldn't be overly stressed. He provided the protection for me that allowed Nancy to be comfortable about my leaving and going back to work. Nancy acknowledged Dakota's gifts and trusted him to protect not only me, but her, too.

At the end, Cody showed me how to die, and that in death, there's freedom and new life. But Dakota isn't dead. He lives on—in the memories of all of those people he touched and in all the awards that he was given; in all the wonderful people who volunteer their time in animal-assisted therapy, sharing unconditional love and helping those who may be sick, lonely, or hurting physically; in all of those people with disabilities who count on a service dog to help them get along in their daily lives; and in cancer patients—humans and animals alike—to remind them that there's always hope.

Cody also lives on in two different Ogilvies—his very special and brilliant veterinarian, Greg, and in his own heir apparent; in Marty Becker, Susan Duncan, and Brenda McClelland; and in organizations such as Delta Society and Therapy Dogs International, all strong advocates for the powers of our animals and the advantages of the human-animal bond.

From Dr. Marty Becker's nomination of Dakota for the Alabama Animal Hall of Fame:

Hey, this wasn't a dog. Dakota was heeler and healer, anxiety reliever and angel, trusted medical sentinel and teacher, fur-covered hot water bottle and friend. Dakota brought all his gifts to bear on behalf of Mike's health and well-being. Dakota jolted Mike out of a sedentary lifestyle and kept him physically and socially active. Dakota provided much-needed comfort and calm to Mike, who was always nervously waiting for the next "cardiac shoe" to drop. Dakota used a gifted sensory system to predict Mike's heart attacks before they occurred, thus allowing Mike a period of grace to find safety or comfort. And last but not least, Dakota provided comfort for the soul to Mike and the rest of his human family.

In Dakota's case, "human family" numbered in the millions, as Dakota became a spokesdog of sorts for the positive effect of pets on human health and well-being. From top television shows and magazines, human hospitals to veterinary clinic waiting rooms, corporate boardrooms to street corners, Dakota was a competent, confident, compassionate messenger for the amazing ability of pets to impact human health in a way that is significant, lasting, and measurable.

— Marty Becker, D.V.M.

Eight years ago, if someone else had told me their own stories about the things that have happened to me, I would never have believed any of it. After all, I'm an engineer, a scientist. I'm accustomed to requiring proof and data for every hypothesis and conjecture.

I can't prove that I saw angels in Cody's eyes the night I nearly died of a heart attack in my bed, but I *did* see them. People doubted what he did for me, that he could really alert me that a heart attack was coming. But that's exactly what he did—and to make his point, he then alerted separately on three of my co-workers, saving even more lives in the process.

Cancer miraculously disappearing? An animal communicator? Dakota appearing to me after his death? There are powers at work here in our universe that we can never comprehend. I don't understand, but I believe . . . because I've seen it all.

From Dr. Greg Ogilvie's nomination of Dakota for the Alabama Animal Hall of Fame:

Dakota and Mike became ambassadors to the world, spreading the word about the importance of animals, especially service dogs in society. These two inseparable friends spanned the continent in a crusade to allow others to find an enriched life through the wonder, warmth, and friendship of companion animals.

When Mike and Dakota's life seemed to be at its very best, Dakota developed cancer. Dakota immediately understood that this diagnosis ripped the cloak of hope from Mike's hands. This wonderful dog accepted chemotherapy and radiation with dignity and a sense of purpose. He knew he had to get better fast to care for and love his closest friend, Mike. After 25 weeks of therapy, the two marched forward with greater vigor, showing others that heart disease and cancer are no match for love and a committed spirit.

The duo touched the lives of hundreds of thousands of people through public appearances, television shows such as *Good Morning America,* and a camp for children with cancer. Few two-legged people have ever had the opportunity to touch the lives and hearts of so many.

Dakota never stopped caring for Mike. Even though Dakota is no longer with Mike physically, he has joined the angels above to watch over Mike, Nancy, and their new service dog, Ogilvie. Dakota embodied the very finest that love, courage, devotion, and life could be. There could be no more deserving creature of this award.

— Gregory K. Ogilvie, D.V.M.

Christmas letter from Dr. Ogilvie:

Dear Mike, Nancy, and Ogilvie:

'Tis a very special time of year . . . Christmas is a season of promise and of pause to remember the magical things of life. You two (three, I meant—sorry, Ogilvie) have entered my life and have made it so wonderful. You have added meaning, magic, texture, and wonder. This note has been difficult to start

and finish, because I know we all miss Dakota terribly . . . he is with us yet again this Christmas in so many ways, as he has been throughout this entire year, even since he has joined the angels. Indeed, distance has not been a barrier . . . he has been with me this year in France, Germany, Italy, South Africa, Japan, Mexico, and several dozen places in the U.S.A., as I have related the magic of this wonderful dog and his people. This coming year, he will once again be with me in France, Belgium, England, Austria, Spain, and America . . . always teaching, caring, and loving others around him. So, this Christmas is a time of promise, pause, celebration. and of reflection. I thank him for bringing you all into my life . . . thank you. Merry Christmas.

    Your friend,

    Always,

    Greg

Dakota continues to live on in me. My work isn't finished, and he tells me to keep going. I'll keep working in his name, to ensure that service dogs and people with disabilities have the same rights of access as everyone else. And I'll keep visiting those who can be helped by the wonderful benefits of interaction with companion animals.

Cody told me how and where to find his replacement: What are the odds that one man in one lifetime would find two animals with this talent? But he also said that no other service animal would do it as well as he did, and that's because of who and what he was. Ogilvie has alerted on me a few times, but he's also missed some episodes. Of course, Ogilvie's personality is much different from Dakota's—Ogilvie entertains Nancy and me and draws our attention away from what troubles us, while Cody was more likely to help us deal calmly and directly with our issues.

I also know of other service animals with the ability to detect impending heart episodes. And so, Susan Duncan of Delta Society and

I hope to set up a foundation in Dakota's name and get funding for a study to discover how these animals know when a heart episode is coming. Through this research, we hope to learn how to train other service animals to detect and alert their partners of impending heart episodes. With God and Cody's help, this research will happen, and many animals will be trained.

Although I was angry with God when He took Dakota, I now understand why it had to happen. I'm thankful that He sent this angel to my family for the time that we had him. But even without Cody, I know that I still have to complete my mission of telling the world about the human-animal bond.

I will always miss Dakota, but I was truly blessed by this four-legged angel. My prayer is that the world will know and understand the love that he and I shared. After all, love is there for each and every one of us, just waiting for us to open our hearts and receive it. Heaven is literally at our feet, looking up at us with loving brown eyes.

■   ■   ■   ■   ■

CHAPTER EIGHTEEN

The Angel

Photo by Gay Glazbrook

An Angel by Your Side

May you always have an angel by your side,
Watching out for you in all the things you do,
Reminding you to keep believing in brighter days,
Finding ways for wishes and dreams
to take you to beautiful places,
Giving you hope that is as certain as the sun,
Giving you the strength of serenity as your guide.
May you always have love and comfort and courage,
And may you always have an angel by your side .

May you always have an angel by your side,
Someone there to catch you if you fall,
Encouraging your dreams,
Inspiring your happiness,
Holding your hand and helping you through it all.
In all of our days, our lives are always changing,
Tears come along as well as smiles.
Along the roads you travel, may the miles be a thousand times
more lovely than lonely,
May they give you the kind of gifts that never, ever end,
Someone wonderful to love and a dear friend
in whom you can confide.
May you have rainbows after every storm,
May you have hopes to keep you warm,
And may you always have an angel by your side.

— Emila Larson

APPENDIX

From the Overview of the Americans with Disabilities Act of 1990 As It Relates to Service Dog Rights

July 26, 1996

The Civil Rights Division of the U.S. Department of Justice and the National Association of Attorneys General have formed a Disability Rights Task Force to promote and protect the rights of individuals with disabilities.

We have found that many businesses across the country have prohibited individuals with disabilities who use service animals from entering their premises, in many instances because of ignorance or confusion about the animal's appropriate use. This document provides specific information about the legal requirements regarding individuals with disabilities who use service animals. It was prepared by the Task Force to assist businesses in complying voluntarily with the Americans with Disabilities Act and applicable state laws.

Twenty-four state attorneys general are distributing a similar document (including state specific requirements) to associations representing restaurants, hotels and motels, and retailers for dissemination to their members.

We encourage you to share this document with businesses and people with disabilities and their families in your community.

Deval L. Patrick
Assistant Attorney General
Civil Rights Division
U.S. Department of Justice

Scott Harshbarger
Attorney General
State of Massachusetts
President, National Association
of Attorneys General

■   ■   ■

COMMONLY ASKED QUESTIONS ABOUT SERVICE ANIMALS IN PLACES OF BUSINESS

Q: What are the laws that apply to my business?

A: Under the Americans with Disabilities Act (ADA), privately owned businesses that serve the public, such as restaurants, hotels, retail stores, taxicabs, theaters, concert halls, and sports facilities, are prohibited from discriminating against individuals with disabilities. The ADA requires these businesses to allow people with disabilities to bring their service animals onto business premises in whatever areas customers are generally allowed.

■　　■　　■

Q: What is a service animal?

A: The ADA defines a service animal as any guide dog, signal dog, or other animal individually trained to provide assistance to an individual with a disability. If they meet this definition, animals are considered service animals under the ADA regardless of whether they have been licensed or certified by a state or local government. Service animals perform some of the functions and tasks that the individual with a disability cannot perform for him or herself. "Seeing eye dogs" are one type of service animal, used by some individuals who are blind. This is the type of service animal with which most people are familiar. But there are service animals that assist persons with other kinds of disabilities in their day-to-day activities. Some examples include:

- Alerting persons with hearing impairments to sounds.

- Pulling wheelchairs or carrying and picking up things for persons with mobility impairments.

- Assisting persons with mobility impairments with balance.

■   ■   ■

Q: How can I tell if an animal is really a service animal and not just a pet?

A: Some, but not all, service animals wear special collars and harnesses. Some, but not all, are licensed or certified and have identification papers. If you are not certain that an animal is a service animal, you may ask the person who has the animal if it is a service animal required because of a disability. However, an individual who is going to a restaurant or theater is not likely to be carrying documentation of his or her medical condition or disability. Therefore, such documentation generally may not be required as a condition for providing service to an individual accompanied by a service animal. Although a number of states have programs to certify service animals, you may not insist on proof of state certification before permitting the service animal to accompany the person with a disability.

■   ■   ■

Q: What must I do when an individual with a service animal comes to my business?

A: The service animal must be permitted to accompany the individual with a disability to all areas of the facility where customers are normally allowed to go. An individual with a service animal may not be segregated from other customers.

■   ■   ■

Q: I have always had a clearly posted "no pets" policy at my establishment. Do I still have to allow service animals in?

A: Yes. A service animal is not a pet. The ADA requires you to modify your "no pets" policy to allow the use of a service animal by a person with a disability. This does not mean you must abandon your "no pets" policy altogether but simply that you must make an exception to your general rule for service animals.

■　　■　　■

Q: My county health department has told me that only a seeing-eye or guide dog has to be admitted. If I follow those regulations, am I violating the ADA?

A: Yes, if you refuse to admit any other type of service animal on the basis of local health department regulations or other state or local laws. The ADA provides greater protection for individuals with disabilities and so it takes priority over the local or state laws or regulations.

■　　■　　■

Q: Can I charge a maintenance or cleaning fee for customers who bring service animals into my business?

A: No. Neither a deposit nor a surcharge may be imposed on an individual with a disability as a condition to allowing a service animal to accompany the individual with a disability, even if deposits are routinely required for pets. However, a public accommodation may charge its customers with disabilities if a service animal causes damage so long as it is the regular practice of the entity to charge non-disabled customers for the same types of damages. For example, a hotel can charge a guest with a disability for the cost of repairing or cleaning furniture damaged by a service animal if it is the hotel's policy to charge when non-disabled guests cause such damage.

■   ■   ■

Q: I operate a private taxicab and I don't want animals in my taxi; they smell, shed hair, and sometimes have "accidents." Am I violating the ADA if I refuse to pick up someone with a service animal?

A: Yes. Taxicab companies may not refuse to provide services to individuals with disabilities. Private taxicab companies are also prohibited from charging higher fares or fees for transporting individuals with disabilities and their service animals than they charge to other persons for the same or equivalent service.

■   ■   ■

Q: Am I responsible for the animal while the person with a disability is in my business?

A: No. The care or supervision of a service animal is solely the responsibility of his or her owner. You are not required to provide care or food or a special location for the animal.

■   ■   ■

Q: What if a service animal barks or growls at other people, or otherwise acts out of control?

A: You may exclude any animal, including a service animal, from your facility when that animal's behavior poses a direct threat to the health or safety of others. For example, any service animal that displays vicious behavior towards other guests or customers may be excluded.

You may not make assumptions, however, about how a particular animal is likely to behave based on your past experience with other animals. Each situation must be considered individually. Although a public accommodation may exclude any service animal that is out of control, it should give the individual with a disability who uses the service animal the option of continuing to enjoy its goods and services without having the service animal on the premises.

■　■　■

Q: Can I exclude an animal that doesn't really seem dangerous but is disruptive to my business?

A: There may be a few circumstances when a public accommodation is not required to accommodate a service animal—that is, when doing so would result in a fundamental alteration to the nature of the business. Generally, this is not likely to occur in restaurants, hotels, retail stores, theaters, concert halls, and sports facilities. But when it does, for example, when a dog barks during a movie, the animal can be excluded.

■　■　■

If you have further questions about service animals or other requirements of the ADA, you may call the U.S. Department of Justice's toll-free ADA Information Line at 800-514-0301 (voice) or 800-514-0383 (TDD). For access problems, contact:

> United States Department of Justice
> 950 Pennsylvania Avenue, NW
> Civil Rights Division
> Disability Rights - NYAVE
> Washington, D.C. 20530

■　■　■　■　■

RESOURCES

Cancer

College of Veterinary Medicine & Biomedical Sciences
Animal Cancer Center
Colorado State University
300 West Drake Road
Fort Collins, CO 80523-1601
(970) 221-4535

The Veterinary Cancer Society: www.vetcancersociety.org
The American College of Veterinary Medicine: www.acvm.org

Other Veterinary Medical Contacts

Dr. Brenda McClelland, D.V.M.
(970) 495-9602
www.energyworkdoctor.com

Dr. Narda Robinson, D.O., D.V.M.
www.aavma.org

Grief Support

Argus Institute for Families and Veterinary Medicine at
Colorado State University: www.argusinstitute.com

Animal-Assisted Therapy, Service Dogs, and Dog Trainers

Delta Society
289 Perimeter Road East
Renton, WA 98055-1329
(425) 226-7357
www.deltasociety.org

Therapy Dogs International
88 Bartley Road
Flanders, NJ 07836
(973) 252-9800
www.tdi-dog.org

The Good Dog Foundation
607 6th Street
Brooklyn, NY 11215
(718) 788-2988
www.thegooddogfoundation.org

Susan L. Duncan, R.N.
Duncan Consulting
Policy, practices & accessibility solutions®
(425) 644-0202
TSMK@msn.com

Association of Pet Dog Trainers
(800) PET-DOGS (800-738-3647)
www.apdt.com

Canine Companions for Independence
P.O. Box 446

Santa Rosa, CA 95402-0446
(866) CCI-DOGS (866-224-3647)
(800) 572-BARK (800-572-2275)
www.caninecompanions.org

Assistance Dogs International, Inc. (ADI)
c/o Canine Partners for Life
230 Whitehorse Road
Cochranville, PA 19330
(610) 869-4902
www.assistance-dog-intl.org

Assistance Dog United Campaign (ADUC)
P.O. Box 2804
Rohnert Park, CA 94927
(800) 284-DOGS

International Association of Assistance Dog Partners (IAADP)
P.O. Box 1326
Sterling Heights, MI 48311
(810) 826-3938
www.iaadp.org

Other Resources

United States Department of Justice
ADA Information & Help
(800) 514-0301 (voice) (800) 514-0383 (TDD)

Guidance Concerning Service Animals/Service Dogs in Air
Transportation (*Federal Register,* Vol. 61, No. 213,
Friday, November 1, 1996, pages 56422–5)

Aviation Consumer Protection
Washington, D.C.
(202) 366-2220

Service & Assistance Dogs Resources Throughout
    The United States and World Guide Dogs, Hearing Dogs,
    Support Dogs
    www.inch.com/~dogs/service.html

Golden Retriever Club of America
National Rescue Committee
www.grca-nrc.org

The American Kennel Club
260 Madison Avenue
New York, NY 10016
(212) 696-8200
www.akc.org

■　　■　　■　　■　　■

ABOUT THE AUTHORS

Michael Lingenfelter is an accomplished engineer and has worked on a number of very visible and important public construction projects in his 40-year career. He has designed and managed construction of communication systems for airports, mass-transit systems, and other public carriers in Dallas, Pittsburgh, Los Angeles, Buffalo, and other cities around the world. A member of the Institute of Electrical and Electronic Engineers and several professional societies, Mike holds 17 patents for his work worldwide. Mike and his wife, Nancy, have four children and seven grandchildren. They reside in Huntsville, Alabama, where Mike is a consultant for Parsons Transportation Group, a division of Parsons Engineering.

David Frei is known to millions of television viewers as the long-time co-host of USA Network's annual telecast of the popular Westminster Kennel Club dog show. He has enjoyed much success in the dog-show world, but he is proudest of the fact that his Brittanys, Teigh and Belle, are registered therapy dogs that visit people in hospitals, nursing homes, and hospices every week. Dave lives in Seattle with his wife, Cherilyn.

Dakota was Mike's very special golden retriever service dog, who possessed unique, life-saving talents, He was named 1999 Service Dog of the Year by Delta Society, elected to the Texas Veterinary Medical Foundation Animal Hall of Fame, chosen as Humanitarian of the Year by the National Sertoma Club of Dallas (the first nonhuman recipient in history), and elected to the Alabama Animal Hall of Fame.

Visit: **www.angelbymyside.com**

We hope you enjoyed this Hay House book.
If you would like to receive a free catalog featuring additional
Hay House books and products, or if you would like information
about the Hay Foundation, please contact:

Hay House, Inc.
P.O. Box 5100
Carlsbad, CA 92018-5100

(760) 431-7695 or **(800) 654-5126**
(760) 431-6948 (fax) or **(800) 650-5115 (fax)**
www.hayhouse.com

■   ■   ■

Published and distributed in Australia by:
Hay House Australia, Ltd. • 18/36 Ralph St. • Alexandria NSW 2015 •
Phone: 612-9669-4299 • *Fax:* 612-9669-4144 • www.hayhouse.com.au

Published and distributed in the United Kingdom by:
Hay House UK, Ltd. • Unit 202, Canalot Studios •
222 Kensal Rd., London W10 5BN • *Phone:* 44-20-8962-1230 •
Fax: 44-20-8962-1239 • www.hayhouse.co.uk

Published and distributed in the Republic of South Africa by:
Hay House SA (Pty), Ltd., P.O. Box 990, Witkoppen 2068 •
Phone/Fax: 2711-7012233 • orders@psdprom.co.za

Distributed in Canada by:
Raincoast • 9050 Shaughnessy St., Vancouver, B.C. V6P 6E5 •
Phone: (604) 323-7100 • *Fax:* (604) 323-2600

■   ■   ■

Sign up via the Hay House USA Website to receive the Hay House online
newsletter and stay informed about what's going on with your favorite
authors. You'll receive bimonthly announcements about: Discounts
and Offers, Special Events, Product Highlights,
Free Excerpts, Giveaways, and more!